The School's on Fire!

The School's on Fire!

A TRUE STORY *of* BRAVERY, TRAGEDY, *and* DETERMINATION

REBECCA C. JONES

CHICAGO REVIEW PRESS

Copyright © 2019 by Rebecca C. Jones
Published by Chicago Review Press Incorporated
814 North Franklin Street
Chicago, Illinois 60610
ISBN 978-0-912777-62-7

Library of Congress Cataloging-in-Publication Data

Names: Jones, Rebecca C., author.
Title: The school's on fire! : a true story of bravery, tragedy, and
    determination / Rebecca C. Jones.
Description: Chicago, Illinois : Chicago Review Press, 2018. | Includes
    bibliographical references and index. | Audience: Age 10 and up. |
    Audience: Grade 4 to 6.
Identifiers: LCCN 2018009633 (print) | LCCN 2018014856 (ebook) | ISBN
    9780912777634 (adobe pdf) | ISBN 9780912777641 (epub) | ISBN
9780912777658
    (kindle) | ISBN 9780912777627 (hardback)
Subjects: LCSH: Our Lady of the Angels School (Chicago, Ill.)—Fire,
    1958—Juvenile literature. | Fires—Illinois—Chicago—Juvenile
    literature. | BISAC: JUVENILE NONFICTION / History / United States / 20th
    Century. | JUVENILE NONFICTION / History / United States / State &
Local.
Classification: LCC LD7501.C434 (ebook) | LCC LD7501.C434 J66 2018 (print) |
    DDC 363.37/650977311—dc23
LC record available at https://lccn.loc.gov/2018009633

Interior design: Sarah Olson

Printed in the United States of America
5 4 3 2 1

*To the kids who survived the fire and
lived with the memories of OLA*

CONTENTS

PROLOGUE

FIRE ALARM!

What kind of fire drill is this?
—Carol Vinceri

It was near the end of the school day on December 1, 1958, and Carol Vinceri was feeling antsy. So when her seventh-grade teacher asked for a volunteer to go downstairs and help a first-grade teacher, Carol quickly raised her hand.

More than half a century later, Carol can't remember exactly what she was doing in the first-grade classroom when she heard the fire alarm. But she clearly remembers everything that happened after that.

Some of the first graders jumped or cried out at the sound of the alarm. Carol had been through so many school fire drills, though, that she knew exactly what to do: she helped the first graders line up at their classroom door, led them out to the hall, and walked quickly toward the school's front door.

Carol was the first person to reach the door, and when she tried to open it, the door seemed stuck. "I had the feeling, when I was trying to get the door open, that somebody was holding it on the other side," she remembers. "But I kept trying and trying, and finally I got it open."

Once outside, Carol led the first graders down the steps, away from the building, and across the street. Then she turned around and faced the school. Looking up to her own seventh-grade classroom on the top floor, she was surprised to see a window pop open and smoke begin to billow out.

Carol stared at the smoke. *Well, that's strange*, she remembers thinking. *What kind of fire drill is this?* She couldn't believe her classroom was filling with real smoke. She decided firemen must have pumped fake smoke into the building to make the fire drill seem more realistic.

Then she moved a few steps so she could see another section of the building. There she saw flames leaping out classroom windows. And kids crying for help. *This isn't pretend*, Carol thought. *This is real.*

This model shows what Our Lady of the Angels School looked like at the time of the fire. The miniature school, made in the early 2000s by Stuart Gootnick of Chicago, now sits in the Fire Museum of Greater Chicago.

It certainly was. Carol's school—Our Lady of the Angels School in Chicago, Illinois—was destroyed on that cold December day, in one of the worst school fires in American history. Carol (and all of the first graders she was helping) escaped without physical injury, but many others did not.

The fire horrified Americans. How could such a thing happen? Weren't schools supposed to be safe?

On the outside, Our Lady of the Angels certainly looked strong and safe. The school used two smaller buildings for kindergartners and some first graders, but most students were in the main building—a sturdy red-brick structure with three floors of classrooms. (Most of the school's 24 classrooms were on the main building's top two floors, but a few were located in a basement that rose a half story above ground level.) The U-shaped building had a narrow courtyard between its north and south wings.

Covering more than half a city block, Our Lady of the Angels was the largest structure in its neighborhood on Chicago's West Side. Indeed, Our Lady of the Angels—or OLA, as it was known in the neighborhood—was one of the largest elementary schools in the country, with more than 1,600 students, from kindergarten through eighth grade.

OLA was a Catholic school near a church with the same name. The vast majority of its students came from families who lived in small apartment buildings and houses within a few blocks of the school and church.

In the middle of the 20th century, Catholic schools were so common in Chicago that one appeared every few blocks. Even people who weren't Catholic often identified their neighborhood by the name of the Catholic church and school closest to their home. With 417 elementary and 93 high schools, the Archdiocese of Chicago ran the third-largest school system in the country, behind New York City Public Schools and Chicago Public Schools. (At the time, Chicago was the second-largest city in the United States.)

Most Catholic schools in Chicago (and other American cities) sprang up in the 19th and 20th centuries to teach the children of European immigrants, who often did not feel comfortable or welcome in public schools. Indeed, many OLA students or their parents were born in other countries, especially Italy, Ireland, and Poland.

There was nothing fancy about OLA in 1958. The school received no money from the government, and most parents paid very low tuition—two or three dollars a month—for their child's education. And parents with large families paid less per child.

The bulk of the school's budget came from church collections and fundraisers. Parents held bake sales and collected old clothes for rummage sales, while kids sold raffle tickets, candy, Christmas cards, and anything else their friends and relatives might buy. Still, the biggest reason for OLA's low tuition was that most of its teachers were nuns who worked for a pittance—and were willing to teach huge classes.

WOMEN IN BLACK

—

Nuns were religious women who never married and who devoted their lives to prayer and service, usually as teachers or nurses. OLA's nuns belonged to a religious order, or community, called Sisters of Charity of the Blessed Virgin Mary—or BVMs for short.

The OLA nuns maintained strict order in very large classes.

BVM nuns wore long black dresses and veils that hid their hair and blocked their side vision. Most BVMs were very strict and kept tight control over their students. The nuns said they had to be strict because their classes were so large. It was not unusual to have 50, 60, or even more kids in a classroom with just one nun.

Many nuns enforced classroom rules gently, sometimes with humor. Some, though, screamed with rage and even hit students. In those classrooms, kids whispered that BVM stood for Black-Veiled Monster.

Like other Catholic schools at the time, OLA displayed crosses in its classrooms and religious statues in its hallways. Otherwise, it looked pretty much like many other public and private schools in midcentury America, with high ceilings, polished wooden staircases, and wide, open hallways.

OLA looked so familiar that when parents around the country later saw pictures of its smoldering remains in their newspapers, they couldn't help but wonder: if a fire could happen at this school, could it also happen at the school their own children attended?

The answer, quite simply, was yes. In fact, two public schools had been destroyed in earlier disasters. A 1908 fire at Lakeview Elementary School in Collinwood, Ohio, killed 178 teachers and students. And a 1937 explosion and fire at a New London, Texas, school killed 427.

But the fire at OLA did something the earlier tragedies had not: it focused Americans' attention on fire safety and led to major changes in how schools (and buildings in general) are built and protected. If your school has fire doors, automatic sprinklers, alarms that connect to the local fire department, or about a dozen other safety features, it's probably because of what happened at Our Lady of the Angels.

So what, exactly, happened at OLA?

THE STAIRWELL

Call the fire department, quick! The school's on fire!
—James Raymond

The fire began quietly in the northeast corner of the school basement. Someone lit three matches and dropped them into a cardboard trash barrel at the bottom of a wooden stairway that was seldom used. Nobody saw who lit the matches, and nobody noticed the small flame as it smoldered for at least 15 or 20 minutes.

In their classrooms, teachers were finishing up lessons and sending kids on end-of-the-day errands. Two boys from each classroom carried wastebaskets down to the school's boiler room. Several older girls went downstairs to help teachers with younger children. One left for her weekly music lesson in the convent across the street. Thirteen eighth graders were also dismissed early so they could help carry old clothes that had been donated for a fundraiser at the church next door.

But most kids were still in their classrooms, looking forward to the dismissal bell. They had no idea that a small flame in a basement trash barrel was growing into a dangerous fire.

The fire continued to grow in the stairwell until its intense heat shattered a window, bringing in a fresh supply of outside air. As oxygen fed the flames, the fire grew even larger.

OLA had extremely large classes, sometimes with as many as 70 students in a single classroom. No matter how many students there were, each classroom had just one teacher, usually a nun.

School janitor James Raymond was probably the first person to discover the fire. He was outside walking toward the school when he thought he smelled smoke.

Puzzled, he looked around until he saw a red light glowing through a basement window. He rushed toward the fire but saw it was already too big to fight by himself.

"I figured it was so big, there was nothing I could do," he said later. "I didn't have nothing with me. Only my two hands. I was worried mainly about getting the children out of the school." Four of his own children were in OLA that day.

He ran to the closest phone, which was in the church rectory, where priests lived, across an alley. He burst into the kitchen and found the housekeeper, fixing a sauce for the priests' dinner.

"Call the fire department, quick!" Mr. Raymond shouted. "The school's on fire!"

Then he ran back to the burning building.

"I dashed into the boiler room, which is right across the way," he later said. "There were two little boys in there, with wastepaper baskets. I told them to drop the baskets and get back. . . . I chased them right out."

Meanwhile, a salesman drove by the school and saw smoke pouring out of the building's basement. He pulled over to the curb and looked for one of the red fire-alarm boxes that allowed people on the street to call local firehouses. (In 1958, no one had cell phones.) When he didn't see a red box, the salesman ran to a nearby candy store and asked to use the telephone.

Store owner Barbara Glowacki didn't feel comfortable letting strangers into her back room to use the phone, so she told him she didn't have a public telephone.

"The school next door is on fire!" the salesman yelled as he rushed out the door to find another phone.

Not sure whether to believe him, Mrs. Glowacki went outside to check. At first she thought the school looked the same way it always did. Then she saw a bright-orange flame through a basement window. She ran inside and called the fire department. "Our Lady of the Angels School is on fire!" she said. "Hurry!"

The emergency operator was calm. "Somebody called it in already," he said. "Help is on the way."

But help did not come immediately. The rectory housekeeper had given the fire department the rectory's address rather the school's address. The rectory was around the corner and about half a block from the fire's location. The first fire truck lost precious minutes going to the wrong address.

Once firemen arrived at the rectory and recognized the mistake, they had to reposition their trucks and hook their hoses to different water hydrants. Even then, they did not have the extra equipment and extra men they would normally take to a building as big as Our Lady of the Angels School.

Inside the school, most of the teachers and students still did not know that anything was wrong. The school's fire alarm had not rung, and everyone continued to follow regular end-of-the-day routines.

But the fire in the basement stairwell was getting bigger. It began climbing—and consuming—the wooden staircase to the school's first floor. A closed door blocked the fire from entering the first-floor hallway and classrooms.

Hungry for oxygen, the fire rushed up another flight of stairs. On the second floor, there were no doors separating the stairs from the hallway. Thick black smoke poured into the corridor and pressed against classroom doors. Meanwhile, hot air and gases inside the basement wall began flowing upward to a shallow space above the second-floor ceiling.

Some kids began to fan themselves. They knew it was cold outside—only 17 degrees Fahrenheit—but their classrooms were getting awfully hot.

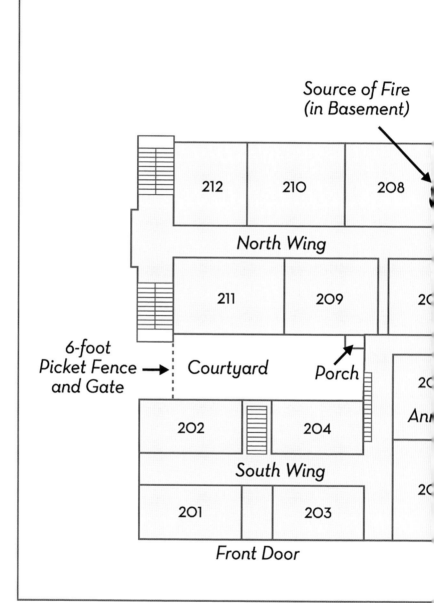

OLA SCHOOL MAP

Source of Fire
(in Basement)

212   210   208

North Wing

211   209   20

6-foot
Picket Fence →   Courtyard   Porch
and Gate

20

20

An

202   204

South Wing

20

201   203

Front Door

This map shows the layout of the top floor of OLA's main building. The fire started in a basement trash can (top right), roared up the stairs, and entered classrooms on the top floor of the north

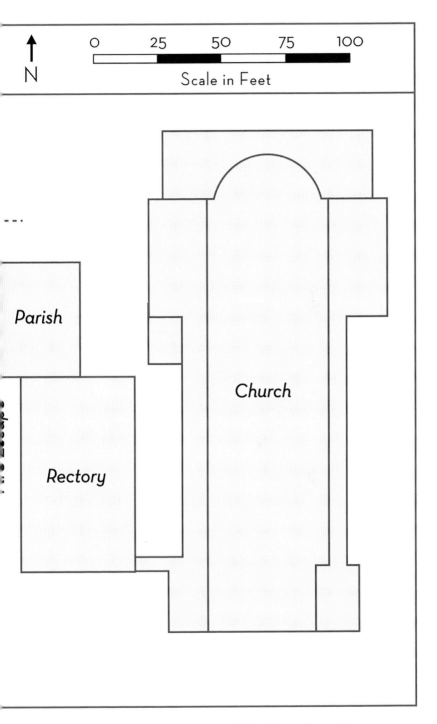

Parish

Rectory

Church

wing. Notice how far the origin of the fire is from the rectory—
where firemen were first directed.

ROOM 208

The heck with this, Sister. I'm getting out of here.
—OLA seventh grader

At the top of the stairs, seventh graders in Room 208 were the first to feel the heat. Eleven-year-old Luci Mordini remembers someone saying, "It's really hot in here. Can we open the transom over the door?" Transoms—small glass windows over classroom doors—were normally kept shut.

The teacher—a gentle, scholarly nun named Sister Mary Saint Canice Lyng, known to her 47 students as Sister St. Canice—gave permission, and a boy pulled a long rod that was supposed to open the transom. But the transom didn't budge.

Then the classroom door began to rattle, like a breeze was shaking it. At first Sister St. Canice thought eighth graders were in the hallway playing with the door handle again. For some reason they liked to do that, and she supposed she would have to correct them again. But when she opened the door, a dense fog of smoke rolled into the room. She immediately slammed the door shut.

The classroom had another door near the back of the room. A boy opened it a crack, but when he saw the black smoke, he slammed that door shut too.

"Then it was like a Steven Spielberg movie," remembers Serge Uccetta (pronounced Surge You-set-ah), who sat in the row of desks closest to the windows. "All of

a sudden, smoke started coming in from the crack between the bottom of the door and the floor. And that was scary."

Serge Uccetta, shown here a few months before the fire, smelled smoke shortly after he returned from taking Room 208's trash down to the boiler room.

Several kids jumped in alarm, and some screamed. Calmly, Sister St. Canice told everyone to sit down. The fire department was surely on its way. In the meantime, she said, they should all pray. She walked up and down the classroom aisles, trying to reassure kids with the light touch of her hand on their shoulders.

The classroom was quiet for a moment as everyone listened for sirens. They didn't hear any, and the room was growing dark with a thick, oily smoke that made breathing difficult. Serge pulled out a handkerchief to cover his mouth and nose.

Another boy stood up. "The heck with this, Sister," the boy said. "I'm getting out of here."

Kids began rushing for the windows. Some taller boys pushed them open, and everyone crowded around, trying to reach the fresh air. The windows were high, about four feet off the floor, and there were only four of them, so it was hard for everyone to find a pocket of air.

Andy Lego, a short boy who sat in the front row, hoisted himself onto one of the window ledges and looked out. He saw flames shooting out the window on the stair landing next to their classroom. "I can still see the flames," Andy says, more than half a century after the fire. "To this day, I close my eyes and see those flames."

Inside the classroom, the air was becoming dense and black. Some seventh graders cried and called for their mothers.

Andy knew he had to get out. He'd always had a terrible fear of heights, but he forced himself to crawl outside onto the window ledge. Behind him, he heard glass shatter—probably the transom over the door—as he let himself down over the ledge. "I hung there by my fingertips for what seemed like 14 hours, but was really about two seconds," he remembers. "And then I let go."

A hard roof over a basement door broke his fall. Andy rolled off and dropped to the ground. His only injury was a sprained ankle. "I was one of the first ones out," he says. "I hit the ground just as neighbors were beginning to bring ladders."

Neighbors who'd seen or smelled the fire were grabbing household ladders and running to the school. Other second-floor windows did not have roofs beneath them. And with the hall and stairs blocked by thick smoke and hungry flames, windows seemed to be the only way out of second-floor classrooms in the north wing. Without a roof or awning to break their falls, most kids faced a 25-foot drop to the alley below.

The neighbors' ladders were far too short to reach the second-floor windows, so some kids began jumping to the alley.

Still holding a handkerchief over his mouth and nose, Serge Uccetta waited at one of the windows for his turn to jump. He watched a boy in front of him jump to the alley and not get up. The boy lay perfectly still.

Then Serge saw Mr. Raymond rushing toward the school with the tall ladder he used for repairs. *Please,* Serge thought, *bring the ladder here—to this window!* He thought about throwing down one of his shoes to get the janitor's attention. But Serge figured he would need both shoes if he had to jump to the alley. So he threw down his glasses.

The glasses caught Mr. Raymond's attention, and he brought the ladder to Serge's window. Although this ladder was taller than most of the ladders neighbors brought, it still wasn't tall enough to reach the second floor. So Serge scrambled out the window and hung from the ledge, just like Andy had done, before letting himself drop to the ladder. He wasn't hurt, but he had to climb down and get out of the way quickly because so many kids were dropping and jumping from windows.

One girl remembers hesitating at a window as she watched boys jump and crack their heads on the alley below. "I thought I was going to die either way because the window sill was burning," she remembers.

Then one of her classmates suggested that they form a human chain to lower themselves to Mr. Raymond's ladder. Kids were pushing and shoving, but she got out of the window and held on to the legs of the boy above her until she dropped safely to the ladder.

Several other kids later said that Sister St. Canice helped them escape. She dropped them to ladders or even pushed them out of windows in an attempt to save them from the deadly fire.

Luci Mordini is not sure how she got out. "I was sitting on the window frame, with my legs out, and I think I was holding onto the window frame," she says. Maybe somebody pushed her out. Or maybe she fell out when the roof collapsed.

Even though she doesn't remember how she got out of Room 208, Luci is pretty sure she did not jump. "There were kids lying on the ground already, and they weren't moving," she remembers. "There were no firemen yet. So I don't think I would have [jumped]. I'm not that brave."

Luci also doesn't remember what happened next because she passed out. "When I woke up, I was already away from the school building and some man was talking to me," she says. She thinks this man took her, along with at least one other kid, to the hospital in his car. "I left for the hospital before any firemen even showed up."

Luci stayed in the hospital for 24 days and spent several months recovering at home. Today she still has

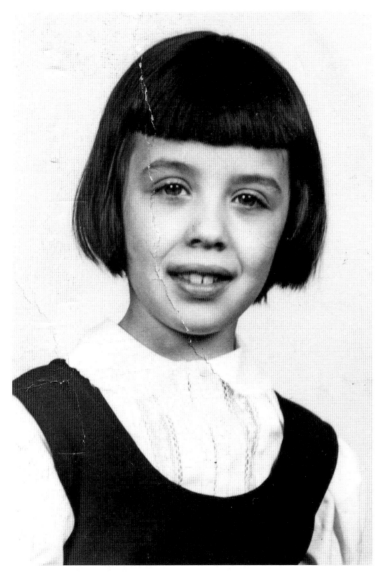

Luci Mordini did not want to jump but might have been thrown off her window perch when the ceiling fell in Room 208.

scars from the burns she got while sitting on that hot windowsill.

But she is alive. Twelve of her classmates died that day. When firemen came into Room 208 later, they found the body of Sister St. Canice, draped protectively over the bodies of several girls. Evidently, firemen said, she had tried to shield them from the fire and its deadly fumes for as long as she could.

ROOM 207:
THE CHEESE BOX

Is this how I'm going to die?
—Kathy Galante

About the time Sister St. Canice first saw smoke
in the second-floor hallway, other people were
seeing and smelling signs of fire too. One of the first
was a girl in a classroom that had been nicknamed the
Cheese Box because of its small size.

Once used as the school library, the Cheese Box was
separated from other classrooms in the north wing by
hallways on three sides. Across the hall and kitty-corner
from Sister Canice's classroom, the Cheese Box held a
combined class of 41 fifth- and sixth-grade students.

The kids in the Cheese Box were all passing quiz papers forward when a girl pointed to the transom over the door.

"Sister," she said, "I see smoke."

Sister Mary Geraldita Ennis—a peppy young nun called Sister Geraldita—moved quickly to the classroom's front door. When she opened it, she saw a wall of flames coming toward the Cheese Box.

She slammed the door and sprinted to the classroom's other door, at the back of the room. This back door—which opened to a short hallway that led to OLA's only fire escape—was always kept locked. Even during fire drills, students never used the fire escape. Instead, they formed a line to march across the hall and down the north wing's back stairs. But those stairs were now filled with flames. Sister Geraldita normally kept the key to the back door on a key ring attached to her belt. But when she looked down at her belt that afternoon, she saw her keys were not there. She had forgotten to bring them to school that day.

Sitting at the desk closest to the back door, 10-year-old Matty Plovanich watched his teacher. "I will never forget the look on her face," he says. "It was complete panic and anguish."

Sister Geraldita leaned against the back door and tried to push it open. When that didn't work, she took several steps back and ran at the door. When that failed too, she enlisted the help of two sixth-grade boys, who were the biggest kids in the class.

The boys stood about 20 paces from the door and followed the nun's instruction to run and throw themselves against the door as hard as they could. They did what she said, but the door did not budge. The boys tried again. Still, the door stood firm.

Then the glass transom over the main door burst. "The smoke really began to billow into the classroom," Matty remembers. "That's when the panic started."

Kids ran to the windows, screaming for help. The Cheese Box had only two windows, which looked down on an empty walkway between the school and the rectory. With the rectory's windows closed against the cold day, no one could hear the kids screaming inside the Cheese Box.

Sister Geraldita picked up a pot of geraniums from her classroom and threw it against the rectory. The crashing sound brought the priests' housekeeper outside.

"Help! Help!" the kids cried. "The school's on fire! We can't get out!"

The housekeeper ran back into the rectory and called Father Charles Hund, a young priest who had gone to bed that afternoon because he wasn't feeling well.

Father Hund came outside, saw the problem, and told the kids to stay there. He said he would get them out.

But the Cheese Box continued to fill with smoke. Sister Geraldita gathered her students around her, near the locked back door. Instructing them to kneel, she led them in the Act of Contrition—a Catholic prayer that expresses sorrow for past sins. Then she led the kids in another Catholic prayer, the Rosary: "Hail Mary, full of grace. Blessed art thou amongst women. . . ."

The steady repetition of familiar prayers quieted the class. Some kids realized that Sister Geraldita was preparing them for their deaths. Later, they described a strange peacefulness that came over them, as if they were being lulled to sleep.

But other kids resisted. One boy ran to a window, jumped out, and landed on the fire escape below. He was obviously hurt (and later needed to be hospitalized), so other kids decided to stay in the Cheese Box.

"I really did not have the guts to jump," Matty Plovanich says. He recalls feeling strangely detached, as if he were watching the scene in his classroom from a distance. In his mind's eye, he also saw another scene, with his parents and his three brothers. They were all sitting around the kitchen table in their apartment, with an empty chair at the place where Matty normally sat. "Their faces were kind of grim and bowed down," he says, "and I felt bad because I knew they were going to miss my presence."

One of his classmates, Kathy Galante, also remembers feeling sadly calm: "I thought to myself, *Is this how I'm going to die?*"

Soon the classroom was filled with so much smoke that kids couldn't see each other or even their own hands. But they still heard Sister Geraldita's voice. Following her instructions, they crouched down until their faces touched the floor, near the last breathable air.

"I had my head down to the floor at the end, and I had my eyes closed," Matty remembers. "I knew the floor was there only because I could feel it. When I opened my eyes, I couldn't see anything, left or right. I mean, I couldn't see anything. It was total darkness."

Meanwhile, Father Hund was running upstairs in the building's south wing and into the smoke-filled north wing. Coughing and praying, he dropped to the floor and crawled on his hands and knees. The heat was so intense that he thought his clothes were going to burn off his back.

When Father Hund reached the Cheese Box, he struggled to open its locked back door. Without a key, though, the door wouldn't budge. On his hands and knees, he tried to create an escape route by knocking out one of the door's panels, but the wood was too thick. "I began to cry and choke because I couldn't get you guys out, and I knew you were trapped," he later told Matty.

Then Father Hund saw the face of Mr. Raymond, crawling through the smoke toward him. The janitor

Matty Plovanich, who considered himself reborn after escaping the Cheese Box, was later number 74 on OLA's football team. The championship-winning team played under the slogan "Let's do it for the 95," a reference to the students and teachers lost in the fire.

had broken a window with his fist to get inside the school. His wrist was bleeding badly, and he was struggling to breathe in the smoky hallway.

"Have you got a key?" Father Hund asked.

Mr. Raymond produced a huge key ring with dozens of keys on it. But Mr. Raymond couldn't see the keys in the smoky hallway, and he had no idea which one belonged to the Cheese Box door. He guessed he would just have to try them all.

The very first key he tried turned out to be the right one. The lock turned, and the door to the Cheese Box opened.

By this time, kids inside the classroom were lying on the floor, close to their last breaths of air. Father Hund and Mr. Raymond moved quickly through the classroom, yanking kids to their feet and pushing them toward the open door to the fire escape.

Sister Geraldita was the last person out of the Cheese Box. As she stepped onto the fire escape, the room exploded into flames.

The kids, now safely outside, watched the explosion in awe. Then they turned their faces toward the sky. "I don't think I ever saw sky so blue or air so clean in my life," Matty says. "It was like I was reborn. It was just amazing."

Sister Geraldita led her class to the church, where she counted heads and told everyone to run straight home. Kathy Galante took off. Even though it was just 17 degrees Fahrenheit outside, she ran eight blocks in her short-sleeved uniform. "The school is on fire!" she screamed. "The school is on fire! The school is on fire!" She kept screaming as she ran up three flights of stairs to her family's apartment and into her mother's arms.

Matty started home too, but he stopped when he rounded the corner of the school. He had assumed the Cheese Box—separated from other classrooms by hallways—was the only room affected by the fire. Now he could see other classrooms on the top floor of the north wing, where kids were hanging out of windows and screaming for help.

"Smoke was just pouring out all over," Matty says. "I remember seeing a pair of gray hands coming to the window and a little gray face through the smoke, trying to get to the window, and then just falling back in. I remember a girl jumping with her hair on fire. They were all landing so badly, and everyone was screaming."

He couldn't bear to watch anymore. He ran the seven blocks to his family's third-floor apartment. When he burst through the door, his mother took in his tussled appearance and assumed he'd been in a fight.

She grabbed Matty by the ear. "Look at you!" she scolded. "You're a mess! Where's your jacket? Where are your books?"

"Mom," Matty said, "the school's on fire."

His mother pinched his ear even harder as she pulled him into the apartment. "Yeah, the school's on fire," she said. "Get in here." Then she caught a whiff of smoke. She looked at Matty's face and realized the grayness around his nostrils did not come from fighting. "Oh, Matty." She took him into her arms.

"The school's on fire," he repeated. "And it's bad."

As the fire grew, smoke poured from the burning school while many kids and their teachers were trapped inside.

ROOM 210

You've got to save yourself, you really do.
—Connie Bellino

ack at the school, the fire was spreading quickly. The other second-floor classrooms in the building's north wing had no fire escapes. The only ways out of those classrooms were through the hallway or out the classroom windows. When teachers saw the smoke in the hallway, they had to decide on their own what to do. Unlike teachers today, they had no cell phones or speaker systems to connect them with anyone outside their classroom.

By the time most teachers looked into the hallway, it was already black with smoke. Nobody wanted to send students into that. Surely, the teachers thought, kids would be safer if they closed their classroom doors and waited for help to arrive. But transoms burst and classrooms filled with smoke before help could arrive. Kids and teachers had to take care of themselves.

In Room 210, several fourth graders smelled smoke before they saw it. They kept telling their teacher—a small, stern nun named Sister Mary Seraphica Kelley—about the smell, but she just said that somebody must be burning leaves outside.

Then a girl screamed and pointed to black smoke coming in through the open transom.

As soon as he saw the smoke, 10-year-old Ronnie Sarno realized the school was on fire, "but I didn't understand the seriousness of it yet," he says. "[I thought] the firemen were going to come put out the fire, and we'd walk out. I recall some kids even laughing about it." They hoped a fire would get them out of school early, and maybe even cancel the next day's classes.

But kids stopped laughing when they saw how fast their classroom was filling with heavy dark smoke. Sister Seraphica walked quickly to the back of the classroom. When she opened the back door, gases from the fire blew her back against the wall.

For a moment the 57 children in Room 210 were stunned. They had never before seen Sister Seraphica lose control. "That's when things really started to get panicky," Ronnie remembers. "It started to get dark. Kids started to scream." They jumped over desks and

Like most of his classmates, 10-year-old Ronnie Sarno did not understand the seriousness of the fire at first.

other kids in their rush to reach the windows. As the room darkened, Ronnie looked around for his nine-year-old sister, Joanne, who was in the same classroom.

Sister Seraphica tried to regain control. She waved her hands and told kids to hush. Then she tried to gather kids around her to pray. Nine-year-old Connie Bellino knelt by her teacher for a few seconds. "Sister was gathering us around her," she remembers, "and we were all sort of kneeling around her. But then we were choking from the smoke, and I never listened that much anyway, so . . . I went right to the window."

The windowsills were chest high for fourth graders, and Connie climbed onto a radiator so she could stick her head out the window. "My knees were killing me because I was kneeling on the radiator, trying to reach up to the window," she remembers. The heat from the radiator burned her knees, and she tried to protect them by pulling her skirt over her knees. That didn't help, though, because the heat from the radiator burned her hands.

By now Room 210 "was crazy, just chaos, with kids jumping on desks," says Ronnie Sarno. "But some kids just sat there. I remember seeing a couple of kids just sitting there." He also saw Sister Seraphica with four or five girls around her. The girls were crying, and Sister Seraphica was trying to comfort them. The room was getting darker by the second. "After that," he says, "I lost sight of the nun."

But he found Joanne. "Somehow my sister and I managed to find each other, and we were standing at the window," he remembers. "We spoke a couple of words. She was crying, and I tried to—I wasn't crying, I was just very scared."

Then he looked up and saw balls of fire on the ceiling. Off in the distance, he heard sirens, but he realized that no one would come in time to save them. "I turned to my sister, and I said, 'We have to jump,'" he remembers. "And she said no, she didn't want to jump."

Some kids were already jumping, and landing in heaps that did not move. From the alley below, the kids in Room 210 could hear adults yelling, "Don't jump! Don't jump!"

Ronnie decided not to jump. But he needed air, so he pressed closer to the window. So many kids were pushing and shoving around the window that he and Joanne got separated. "We were standing at the window, and it just got so chaotic," Ronnie remembers. "I think, at the end, that we just lost contact, in all the chaos."

As everyone pushed toward the window for air, Ronnie noticed the wooden windowsill was so hot that it was smoking, even though it was not yet on fire. In the crush of bodies, he's not sure what happened next.

One moment he was struggling for air inside the classroom, and the next moment he was outside, tumbling toward the alley below.

"I don't know whether I was pushed out or whether I pushed myself out," he says. "I think I did a somersault on the way down or turned around. I don't know what I did. But I hit the ground, and I landed on my back."

Connie Bellino doesn't remember exactly how she got out, either. "Part of me thinks I did it by myself," she says, "and part of me thinks, *How did I do that by myself?* I must have had help." By then, firemen had arrived, and Connie guesses one might have grabbed her and set her on a ladder.

The next thing she remembers, she was on a ladder, with her hair on fire. A fireman turned his hose on her, and the hard rush of water knocked Connie off the ladder. One of the parents in the alley caught her. She was taken to a hospital, where a nurse bandaged her burned hands and told her, "You have no idea how lucky you are."

Twenty-eight fourth graders—including Ronnie Sarno's sister, Joanne—died with Sister Seraphica in Room 210. Ronnie's older brother, Billy, died in another classroom.

After the fire, some people criticized Sister Seraphica for gathering children around her to pray. But Ronnie thinks she was a hero. "She told the kids to pray," he remembers. "What else is she going to say? 'Jump around the windows because we're trapped?' She did the best she could. The last time I saw her, she had kids around her, and she was trying to comfort them."

But Connie Bellino, who left Sister Seraphica's prayer circle, took a different lesson from the experience. "God helps those who help themselves," she says. "You've got to save yourself, you really do. You've got to think: How am I going to get out of this situation? Anything happens, I'll be the first one running."

ROOM 209

It didn't seem life threatening at the time.
—Andy D'Amore

Across the hall in Room 209, 62 eighth graders had been finishing up a math class when a boy sitting in the back of the room decided it was just too hot. "Sister!" he called to Sister Mary Davidis Devine, who was seated at her desk in the front of the classroom. "It's hotter than hell back here!"

From her own seat in the middle of the room, 13-year-old Rosemary Pisani couldn't believe she'd heard the boy right. *Nobody says "hell" to a nun,* she thought. But Sister Davidis must have been feeling the heat too. "OK," she said, "open the door."

When the boy opened the door, clouds of smoke billowed in. He quickly shut the door.

Sister Davidis tried the door at the front of the classroom, but she saw at once that the hallway was filling with oily black smoke. She had no idea where the smoke was coming from, so she slammed the door shut and thought fast. "OK, everybody," she said. "Throw your math books at the doors. Let's stuff them under the cracks."

A few boys helped their teacher stuff the math books in the spaces under the doors. The other kids stayed in their seats and watched with interest. "I don't remember being frightened or nervous," says Andy D'Amore, who was then 13. "It didn't seem life threatening at the time."

Not everyone remained calm. Rosemary remembers one girl began screaming hysterically. Sister Davidis slapped her across the face—not hard, Rosemary says, but it was enough to quiet the girl. "Sister did not want everyone getting hysterical and crying."

Sister Davidis led the class in a quick prayer, then ordered everyone to the windows. Some boys pushed them open so kids could gulp in fresh air. Across the narrow courtyard, they saw other kids still in their classrooms, unaware of the smoke spreading throughout the building.

Rosemary Pisani felt she grew up a lot after the fire. When her mother didn't like Rosemary's school picture that year, she had this photo taken at a local studio.

"Call to them!" Sister Davidis said.

The eighth graders began yelling, "The school's on fire! The school's on fire!" They threw pencils at the windows across the courtyard, trying to get someone's attention.

A girl in one of those targeted classrooms remembers glancing across the courtyard and wondering what on earth the kids in Sister Davidis's class were doing. Were they having some kind of party?

It was definitely no party. Despite the math books shoved under the door, the classroom was filling with suffocating dark smoke. The glass transoms over the doors burst, and even more smoke rushed into Room 209.

Students pressed closer to the windows. But with 62 kids vying for space at four windows, there were too many people, not enough windows, and definitely not enough fresh air.

At the back window, a group of about 10 kids came up with a way to take turns at breathing fresh air. They formed a loose circle that moved around the window. When kids came close to the window, they stuck their heads out and breathed in fresh air. Then they held their breaths as they moved away from the window and gave other kids their turns at the fresh air.

Elsewhere, Room 209 wasn't so orderly. Some survivors recall their classmates yelling for help, jumping

over desks, and breaking windows. One boy jumped
out a window, landed on a small roof that jutted out
from the first floor, then let himself drop to the cement
below. Others crouched in fear under their desks or
beneath windows. But the walls of the classroom were
catching fire, and kids realized they couldn't stay in
their classroom much longer.

Another boy jumped out a window, then another. But
in the circle moving around the back window, 13-year-
old Jeannie Hart didn't even consider jumping. "In my
brain, I just didn't think I could jump," she remembers. "I
thought I would kill myself." So she kept circling the back
window and taking her turn at breathing in fresh air.

Meanwhile, a man named Sam Tortorice (pronounced Tort-or-REE-see), whose two daughters went
to OLA, was coming home from the grocery store. He
thought he smelled burning wood, looked around, and
saw clouds of smoke coming from the school.

Mr. Tortorice realized some of the smoke was coming
from Room 209, where his daughter Rose was in Sister
Davidis's class. When he looked more closely, he thought
he saw Rose's worried face at one of the windows.

"Rose, wait!" he yelled. "I'm coming!"

He dropped his grocery bags and ran across the
street to one of the school's side doors. Once inside,
he bounded up the stairs and down a hallway. When

smoke kept him from getting any closer, he dropped to the floor and crawled. When he couldn't go any farther, even on his hands and knees, he stood up and pushed open a window at the end of a hallway, not far from the back-corner window in Room 209.

Mr. Tortorice swung one leg over the window ledge and leaned out. Straddling the ledge, he could see, but not reach, the kids in Room 209. Rose was at a window near the middle of the room, nowhere near him.

"Rose!" he shouted. "Come here!"

As Rose began working her way toward the back window, her father looked for some way to reach her. If only the two corner windows were closer, he could reach in and pluck her—and everyone else—out of that burning room. But the windows were several yards apart, 25 feet above the concrete courtyard. The kids couldn't walk on thin air, and there was no ledge, not even a narrow one, that connected the two windows. There was nothing but two flat brick walls.

And a rain gutter.

At the very top of the brick walls, right under the roof, Mr. Tortorice spotted a simple gutter that was designed to carry rainwater off the school's roof. He motioned for kids to grab the gutter and swing themselves, as if the gutter were a monkey bar, to the corner of the building and then to his window.

Sister Davidis saw what he meant and began boosting kids out the back window of her classroom. Jeannie Hart—who'd been afraid to jump out the window—was one of the first to try. What propelled Jeannie were the flames now in the classroom. "When the wall a couple of feet away from me was on fire," she remembers, "I knew I had to go *now*."

Other kids pressed toward the back window, and a few—including Rose Tortorice—went before Jeannie. Sister Davidis helped her students out the window at a steady pace, urging some to go faster and others to slow down. She wanted to keep three or four kids on the rain gutter at a time. Any more than that, and she feared the gutter might break. Any fewer, and not enough kids would get out.

While Jeannie waited her turn at the window, she saw a fire truck pull up to the gate in front of the school's courtyard. The gate was locked, and parents were there, crying and calling to their children through the iron fence that separated the sidewalk from the courtyard. The parents pushed and pulled, but no matter what they did, they couldn't get past the locked gate.

When the fire truck arrived, firemen jumped out of the truck and joined the parents in trying to open the locked gate. "The fire truck was right there," Jeannie remembers, "so I'm sure some kids thought, 'The firemen will come and save me.' . . . That's not what happened in my brain. In my brain, I had to get out."

Finally it was her turn to crawl out of the window. Sister Davidis boosted Jeannie up so she could stand on the narrow cement sill outside the building. With Sister holding her legs, Jeannie turned around so she was facing the building. Then she jumped up and reached for the gutter.

"If I missed the rain gutter," Jeannie says, "I may or may not have landed on the window sill again. I may have dropped. I don't know. . . . Thank goodness as a kid, I'd been a little bit tomboyish and done a lot of climbing and all of that."

She grabbed the gutter and dangled from it for just a moment. Then she pulled herself with her hands about six feet to the inside corner of the building. She turned the corner and pulled herself, again by her hands, the last few feet to the window, where Mr. Tortorice reached out to grab her. He swung her into the smoky hallway.

Jeannie dashed across the hall and down the stairs to an outside exit. On the way down, she saw a young priest, Father Joseph Ognibene [pronounced Ahg-nib-BAY-knee], galloping up the stairs to help Mr. Tortorice.

When Father Ognibene arrived, Mr. Tortorice repositioned himself so the two men could get more

Jeannie Hart, shown here at her eighth-grade graduation cel-
ebration several months after the fire.

students out faster, without having them dangle from
the rain gutter. Mr. Tortorice stood on a small first-floor
awning and grabbed kids who jumped to him from the
back window. (One of the kids he caught was Rosemary

Pisani, the girl who had been surprised to hear a boy say "hell" to a nun.) He swung the kids to Father Ognibene, who was leaning out the hallway window. Together, the two men rescued more than 20 kids.

Other kids either jumped or fell out of windows while firemen continued to struggle with the locked gate. Finally, the firemen attached a chain to the gate and pulled it down with a fire truck. The men then raced into the courtyard and threw ladders up against the building.

They reached Room 209 in time to pull out the last few kids, who were badly burned but alive. Sister Davidis insisted on staying in the classroom until she felt sure all of her students were out. A fireman finally carried her out of the room.

As they started down the ladder, Sister Davidis looked back and saw one of her students, Beverly Burda, lying unconscious on the floor near her desk. The nun tried to go back for Beverly, but the fireman stopped her. There simply wasn't time. They were still on the ladder when the ceiling of Room 209 crashed down in flames.

Another girl from Room 209—Valerie Thoma—later died in the hospital from burns and injuries.

As tragic as those deaths were, survivors still marvel that 60 kids got out of Room 209. They credit the men at the window and their quick-thinking teacher.

Jeannie Hart, who later became a teacher herself, is particularly impressed with what Sister Davidis did. "In that moment, to keep things calm and to not lose more of us," she says, "is absolutely unbelievable."

But a very different story was unfolding in the classroom next door.

ROOM 211

I wiggled like a snake to get out from
under the mass of bodies.
—John Lubke

The eighth graders in Room 211 had heard about the fire early. Three girls had returned from an errand shortly before 2:30 and told their teacher that there was smoke in the hall.

The teacher—a hefty nun named Sister Mary St. Helaine O'Neill—did not like surprises. She liked being in charge, and kids knew she did not accept challenges to her authority kindly. Behind her back, they called her Sister Mary Hurricane.

Sister St. Helaine considered the girls' report. A smoky hallway did not fit into her plans for the end of the school day. She had just sent 13 boys off to help carry boxes for the church's annual clothing drive. She didn't need any more interruptions.

Near the back of the classroom sat 13-year-old Eddie Glanz, who liked interruptions. He had volunteered to help carry boxes for the clothing drive at church—anything to get out of school early—but Sister hadn't picked him. So he was sitting near the classroom's back door when the girls came in and reported smoke in the hallway. "Obviously, it wasn't a real heavy smoke because they'd just walked down the hall," he remembers. "It was just kind of a haze."

A few minutes later, two boys came in from cleaning erasers. Smoke billowed in with them, and one of the boys said, "Sister, the school is on fire!"

This time Sister St. Helaine went to the door. Already the door handle was too hot to touch with her bare hands, so she used her long black skirt like a potholder to turn the knob. She looked into the smoky hall and decided to keep her students in the classroom.

This would prove to be a mistake.

After the fire, many survivors pointed out that Room 211's front door was just a few steps from the school's front staircase, which was safe at the time. (The boys had just brought the erasers up these stairs.) If the 48 students then in Room 211 had left their classroom when smoke was first reported, they all could have hurried down the stairs and gotten out safely. Or at least that's what many people said after the fire.

At the time, though, Sister St. Helaine didn't know where the smoke in the hallway was coming from. And she hadn't heard a fire alarm.

So she closed the door and led everyone in a quick prayer. Then, as smoke began to seep into the classroom, she sent kids to the windows.

Thirteen-year-old John Lubke was the first to reach the front window. He pushed it open and lay on the windowsill so the top half of his body was hanging outside and the bottom half was still in the classroom. Other kids piled on top of him. John remembers they piled up "like cords of wood, all trying to get some air."

On the street below, John watched the same crying parents and struggling firemen that other trapped kids saw. And when the fire truck finally pulled down the locked gate, he felt the same surge of relief as everyone else. As the firemen raced into the courtyard and threw ladders against the building, John remembers thinking, *Ah, the firemen are here! We're saved!*

But most of the ladders weren't tall enough to reach the windows in Room 211. "Their freaking ladders were too short," John says. "They couldn't reach us!"

Because firemen had thought they were coming to a house fire at the rectory, most of the ladders they first brought did not reach all the way to the top floor of OLA. Only one ladder was tall enough to reach one window in Room 211. The firemen did not place it at John's window.

As flames roared into the room, John knew he could not wait for another ladder on another truck. "I felt my rear end getting hot," he remembers. He knew he had to take care of himself. "So I wiggled like a snake to get out from under the mass of bodies. I just *wiggled*," he says. Finally he broke away from the other kids and somersaulted through the air before bouncing three times on the pavement in the school courtyard. Then he passed out.

When he woke up, a priest was praying over him. "I wake up, pass out, wake up, pass out," John remembers. "Then I woke up in an ambulance. Then I woke up in a hospital bed."

John's back and elbow were injured. But he was alive and out of Room 211.

Even after more firemen arrived, not all of the ladders reached the windows on the top floor. Some were still too short.

Other kids struggled to get out too. Thirteen-year-old Michele Barale had not joined the first race to the windows. She had stayed at her desk, near the middle of the room. It was hard for her to believe this was a real emergency. *This can't be happening*, she remembers thinking. *Schools don't burn down. Who ever heard of a school burning down?*

Then the overhead lights began exploding. "Cover your heads!" Sister St. Helaine shouted. "Cover your necks!"

With glass showering down on her, Michele put her hands over her head and rushed toward the windows. But so many kids were crowding around them that there was no room for Michele. "There were all the big, tall guys—*boys*—at the windows," she remembers, and she couldn't squeeze in. So she hitched herself up on a nearby radiator and tried to hold her breath.

Michele knew she couldn't stay on the radiator. It was getting too hot, and she needed air. So she returned to the window. It wasn't as crowded this time. Evidently some kids had passed out from lack of air.

Michele was beginning to feel faint herself. Just as she started to fall, she felt someone grab her. It was Sister St. Helaine. "She grabbed me, held me against her, and put her veil around my face to try to filter out some of the smoke," Michele remembers. Sister held another kid with her other arm. "She was a large, bulky woman," Michele says. "She was tall, and she was wide. It was like being held in a grip of iron." Michele didn't move. "I was still afraid of her, even in the midst of all of that."

Eventually, Sister St. Helaine loosened her grip, and Michele saw the walls of her classroom burning. *I have to get out of here*, she thought.

She climbed over other kids to reach a window. When she got there, she saw a burly fireman coming up the ladder toward her. He saw her, too, and the determined look on her face.

"Wait for me!" he shouted. "I'm coming!"

I'm not waiting for anybody, Michele thought. She set her eyes on the ground, 25 feet below. That's where she wanted to be. She launched herself out the window and into the air.

The fireman—Lieutenant Charles Kamin—reached out and caught her in midair. With one arm around her ribs, he staggered down the ladder and set Michele safely on the ground. Then he hurried back up the ladder. The fire seemed calmer now, and he knew from experience that the kids in Room 211 didn't have much time.

The street in front of the school became clogged with emergency vehicles, firemen, onlookers, and people searching for their families.

By the time Lieutenant Kamin appeared at his window, Eddie Glanz was standing in the front row of kids. Eddie had already decided not to jump, but now with the big fireman blocking the window, he couldn't have jumped even if he had wanted to.

Kids were packed so tightly at the window that Lieutenant Kamin had trouble pulling them apart to get them out. He managed to pluck out some boys by grabbing their belts and dropping them onto his ladder. He didn't have time to take them down to the ground. He wanted to get as many kids out of that room as fast as he could.

He worked faster and faster. At one point he thrust his big arm into the crowd at the window and told kids to grab it. Eddie grabbed his arm and held on. Lieutenant Kamin tried to pull him out, but too many kids were squeezing in on Eddie. He was stuck.

The fireman tried to shake Eddie loose so he could get other kids, but Eddie held on tight and kicked his legs to break away from the others. Lieutenant Kamin yanked Eddie out and swung him around to the ladder. Eddie scurried down the ladder and across the street. When he looked back, he saw flames shooting out the window where he had been standing less than a minute before.

Twenty-four kids got out of the classroom. Sister St. Helaine got out too—although she was badly burned and could never remember how she escaped. Another 24 kids died in Room 211, including two of the three girls who had first reported smoke in the hallway.

ROOM 212

I could hear all of the kids calling for Sister and calling for their mothers. Mostly their mothers.
—John Raymond

cross the hall, the fifth graders in Room 212 had no warning about the smoky hallway or approaching fire. When 10-year-old Johnna Mass Uting first saw smoke through the transom over Room 212, she thought it was fake.

Oh, those firemen!, she remembers thinking. *They're playing a trick on us. They're trying to scare us!* Firemen had come to OLA for fire drills in the past, and Johnna figured they were now testing kids, to see what they would do if they saw something that looked like smoke.

As Johnna calmly closed her geography book, a boy opened the classroom's back door to see what was going on. Black smoke rushed in, and Johnna realized this was not a fake fire. Stunned, she thought, *This is the real thing.*

WHY WAS EVERYONE SO SURPRISED?

——

By the time the fire reached Room 212, didn't kids know about the fire? Hadn't they heard the panic in other classrooms?

The short answer is no. Once the fire got up to the second floor, it moved at terrific speed. It burst into classroom after classroom, just seconds apart. At first, "there was not a lot of screaming in the rooms because the nuns kept people under control," says John Raymond, a survivor from Room 212. By the time the screaming started, kids were so caught up in their own survival that they probably ignored sounds from other classrooms.

The teacher—a young nun named Sister Mary Clare Therese Champagne—ran to the back door and slammed it shut. But the door, which often didn't latch properly, swung open again. Sister used her long skirt to grab the hot doorknob and hold the door shut.

"Everybody stay in your seats," she told her fifth graders. Then she led them in a quick prayer and assured them that firemen were on their way. Johnna stayed in her seat, nervously watching the smoke behind the transoms above the classroom's two doors. As more smoke seeped into the room, kids began coughing.

Still holding the back door shut, Sister Mary Clare Therese told everyone to go to the windows for air. A few of the bigger boys opened the windows, and kids jostled for places where they could breathe in the cold air. But with 54 kids in class that day, there wasn't room for everyone, and some students hesitated.

Johnna stood by her desk and yelled, "Sister! Sister! What do I do?"

Sister Mary Claire Therese called back, "Johnna, get to the window and save yourself!"

By now smoke was billowing across the classroom. "The heat was so intense that it was like you were putting your hand in a campsite flame," Johnna remembers. "I mean, it was so burning *hot!*" Heat singed her hair as she ducked beneath clouds of smoke and worked her way toward a window.

Once she got there, so many kids were crammed together around the window that Johnna felt like she couldn't breathe. Choking, she pulled another kid's head back so she could stick her own head out the window. "I felt a real cold breath of fresh air filling my lungs," she remembers.

Somehow—she doesn't remember how—she got out the window. "The next thing I remember," she says, "is hanging from the ledge on the outside."

Johnna tried to hang on to the window ledge, but she felt the school's brick wall getting hotter. It reminded her of an old movie she'd seen on TV. In the movie, actor James Cagney was hanging from the side of a burning building when it collapsed. Johnna was sure her school building was going to collapse too. "All I could think was . . . it's going to kill me, just like it killed James Cagney. I'm going to collapse with this wall, and it's going to kill me, or the flames will get me," Johnna remembers. "So I said 'OK,' and I let go."

Johnna dropped 25 feet to the gravel part of the alley. As soon as she landed, her right ankle began to swell. She later learned she had broken five bones in her ankle.

But at least she was out of Room 212. Inside the classroom, other kids were still struggling for air.

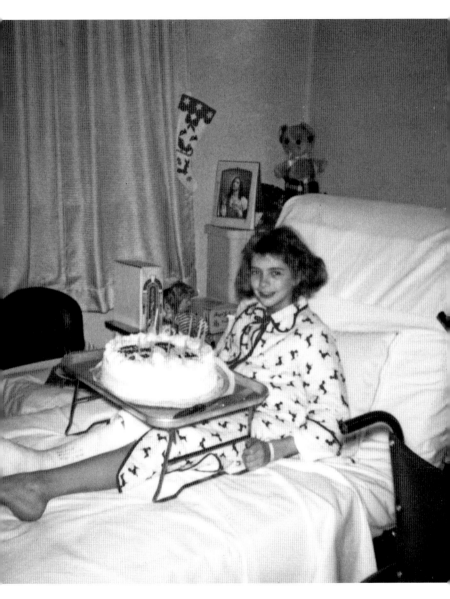

Johnna Mass Uting celebrated her 11th birthday in the hospital, with five broken bones in her right ankle.

Like Johnna, 11-year-old John Raymond had trouble believing this was a real fire at first. Why hadn't he heard the school's fire alarm?

Maybe this wasn't a fire, he thought. Maybe the school's furnace had just backed up. John knew a little about furnaces because he often helped his dad, janitor Jim Raymond, stoke the school and church furnaces at night. What he didn't know was that the school's furnace was not the type that backed up.

John stayed at his desk and did not join the stampede to the windows. "I just sat there," he remembers. "The kid in front of me was there too. I could see his white shirt." Stunned, the two boys did not talk.

The room got darker until John could no longer see the white shirt. "At some point," he says, "I decided I'd better get out."

When John stood up and headed for the front of the classroom, he tripped over something in the darkness. "I never could figure out what made me fall to the floor," he says. "All I know is that I ended up on the floor, and when I was down on the floor, there was air. I crawled to the front, and I could hear all of the kids calling for Sister and calling for their mothers. Mostly their mothers."

Suddenly he felt intense heat on his face. "I must have taken a breath or two of that because then I started having trouble breathing, even though I was down low on the floor." *Please, God, help me*, he prayed. *Please, God, help me.* "I kept saying that—many, many times," John says. "I don't know how many, but I was ready to pass out."

Then, in a move that still surprises him, he stood upright. "I basically panicked," he says. "I pushed anybody and everybody out of the way and dove out the window." Just before he dove, he heard the school's fire alarm.

Looking back, John still feels guilt about pushing other kids. "Some kids probably never got up again because of what I did to them, grabbing them and pulling them out of the way," he says. "It wasn't an act of bravery. It was an act of desperation."

He dove headfirst toward the alley but somersaulted in the air. "I remember falling and thinking how wonderful the cool air felt," he says. "I could breathe. And then I felt the jolt." John landed on his side and injured—but did not break—his back and hip. He was hospitalized for a week.

Altogether, 29 fifth graders escaped the classroom. But young Sister Mary Claire Therese and 26 of her students died in the fire.

THE ANNEX

Half the building was on fire, and half of the
building didn't know what was going on.
—Michael Ramelli

By the time John Raymond—or anyone else—
heard the fire alarm, some kids in the north wing
of Our Lady of the Angels were already on their way to
the hospital. Or dead.

Why didn't the alarm ring sooner? Shouldn't it have
rung at the first whiff of smoke?

Yes, it should have. Seconds really do count in a fire.
(See "What to Do in Case of Fire" on page 129.)

But OLA had no smoke detectors—only two old-
fashioned alarms that required someone to pull a lever.

Both alarms were in the south wing of the building. There was no fire alarm in the north wing, where the fire started. And there wasn't one in the annex, the narrow section of the school that connected the north and south wings.

In one of the annex's two classrooms, 24-year-old Pearl Tristano was finishing lessons with her fifth graders when one of her students reported smoke in the hallway. When Miss Tristano went out to the hall to check for herself, she saw and smelled what he was talking about. She ordered the boy into the classroom, shut the door, and thought about what to do.

She knew OLA had a firm rule about the school's two fire alarms. No one but the principal, Sister Mary St. Florence Casey, was allowed to pull a fire alarm lever. (This rule was supposed to keep pranksters from setting off false alarms to get out of school.) And classes were not allowed to leave the building unless the fire alarm rang.

Miss Tristano, one of the few lay—that is, not a nun—teachers at OLA, hesitated to break firm school rules. But when she saw the smoke in the hallway, she knew she needed to do *something*. So she told her students to stay in their seats while she checked with the teacher in the classroom next door.

Dorothy Coughlan, also a lay teacher, taught sixth grade next door in Room 205. She and Miss Tristano agreed they should notify the principal, who could then sound the alarm. Mrs. Coughlan told Miss Tristano to watch both classes while she went downstairs to Sister St. Florence's office.

But the principal's office was empty. (Sister St. Florence was substituting for a sick teacher in another classroom.) Mrs. Coughlan hurried back upstairs, where she and Miss Tristano agreed to forget the school rules and get their students out of the building. They quickly lined up the kids and led them into the hallway. The smoke was thicker now, but they could see the north wing across the courtyard through the hallway windows.

Michael Ramelli, then 11, remembers seeing smoke and kids at the second-floor windows in the north wing. On the floor below, no one seemed aware that anything was wrong. "I vividly remember a first-grade teacher teaching in a classroom [on the first floor]," he says. "Half the building was on fire, and half of the building didn't know what was going on."

Michael followed his classmates to a staircase in the south wing. As they hurried down the steps and out the door, several kids remember seeing Miss Tristano pull the lever on a fire alarm. But she evidently wasn't sure whether the alarm rang. Once she got her class safely to the nearby church, she ran back inside the school and pulled the alarm again.

For most of the 1,200 kids in the building that day, that fire alarm was their first clue that something was wrong.

THE REST OF
THE BUILDING

My dad didn't know whether to hit me or hug me.
—Johnnie Montedore

The fire alarm surprised almost everyone. Even kids just one floor below the burning classrooms had no idea that the building was on fire.

When the alarm rang, most teachers lined up their kids and filed them out of the school, the way they always did during fire drills. But some teachers and even kids knew at once that this was no ordinary drill. Their big clue: by the time the alarm rang, it was around 2:45, so close to the end of the school day that there wouldn't be enough time to get everyone out of the building and back inside in time for dismissal at 3:00.

When Danny Plovanich's first-grade teacher heard the alarm, she cried, "Oh, my God! It's a fire!"

That was enough for Danny, then six years old and "still a little unsure of fire drill procedures." While his teacher lined up the rest of the class, Danny took off. His desk was right next to the classroom door, he says, "and I guess I didn't see any point in hanging around."

He ran down the hallway and out the front door. He thought he'd be the first person out of the building, so he was surprised to see other kids outside already.

While his teacher hurried the rest of her first-grade class out of the school and over to the warm church, Danny stood outside in his shirtsleeves and watched the excitement unfold around him. "I was a little kid, who knows how tall I was, watching all this chaos swirl around me, as people ran here and there," he remembers. He saw firemen jump off their trucks and stretch out hoses in a "chaotic pattern of lines on the street, like some wild game of pick-up sticks."

He watched smoke—and kids—rush out of the building. One girl ran past him with her hair on fire. "I remember thinking she should stop running because the wind will make her hair catch even more on fire," he says.

Danny Plovanich was Matty Plovanich's little brother and in the first grade when he heard the fire alarm and ran from the building.

Eventually a man spotted Danny and offered him a ride home. Too frightened to speak, Danny decided the offer must be coming from "a bad man because he wanted me to get in his car with him." A woman standing nearby said the nuns were gathering up stray children and taking them to houses in the neighborhood.

"The next thing I remember," says Danny, "is staring out a living room window, looking at news crews on the street, and wondering if I was going to be on TV."

Meanwhile, older kids were still struggling to get out of the building. Seventy seventh graders had been in Room 201 when the fire alarm rang. The classroom's location on the top floor of OLA's south wing meant it was about as far as possible from the north wing basement where the fire had started.

Sitting in the back row next to the windows in Room 201, 12-year-old Mike Guzaldo saw smoke snaking up from radiator pipes. Puzzled, he glanced at the door to the hallway. There didn't seem to be any smoke out there. So he went back to listening to a story his teacher was telling about Joan of Arc.

Sister Mary Andrienne Carolan never finished the story. When the fire alarm rang, the small nun immediately sent her 70 seventh graders into the hall. Smoke was already filling the corridor, and so were other kids. They shoved their way into the hall from other classrooms and started what one kid would later call a "stampede-shuffle" toward the stairs.

Mike Guzaldo was seated close to the door when he first spotted smoke curling up from the radiator pipes in Room 201.

The smoke was getting so thick that 13-year-old Johnnie Montedore, also in Sister Andrienne's class, could hardly see the big globe lights that hung overhead. "You could barely see a glimmer that indicated something was up there; it certainly didn't shed any light at all," he remembers. "It was really pitch black. You could hardly see someone a foot in front of you."

When some kids complained that they couldn't see where they were going, Sister Andrienne yelled for them to hold hands and lead each other toward the stairs. The hallway was becoming chaotic, and Johnnie remembers kids "pushing, shoving, hollering, screaming, and pulling hair." A few kids fell, and Johnnie knows he accidentally stepped on someone's head.

When he reached the stairs, he almost stumbled but couldn't fall, because kids were packed so closely together. "It was just too tight to fall over sideways," he says.

In the scramble down the stairs, Johnnie lost a shoe. "I immediately thought, *My dad is going to kill me*, because they were brand-new shoes." He tried to hold others back with one hand while he felt around for his shoe. But the crowd pushed him along.

Once outside, Johnnie ran with other kids to a water fountain in the nearby rectory. After they gulped down water, some kids giggled and said, "Ooh, we're not going back to this school for a while!" The idea of missing school seemed fun. They didn't know yet about the kids who'd been trapped on the north wing's second floor. They didn't even know about their own classmates still trapped in Room 201.

Sister Andrienne had *thought* everyone was out of the classroom when she joined the throng heading down the stairs. But in the chaos outside the building, she could find dozens of her students, but not all 70 of them.

When she looked up to Room 201's windows, she was horrified to see several familiar faces calling for help. (She later learned someone had slammed shut one of the classroom's two doors, and someone else had panicked and blocked others from leaving.)

Sister Andrienne charged back into the building, up the stairs, and into her classroom, where some students were becoming disoriented in the thick smoke. She ordered them down on their hands and knees, told them to grab the hem of her skirt, and led them on a crawl to the stairway. When some kids hesitated at the top of the stairs, she pushed them so they rolled down the steps.

She returned to the classroom several times to lead more crawling students to the stairway. Meanwhile, firemen and even neighbors placed ladders at the classroom windows and brought others down to safety. At last, all of Sister Andrienne's students were outside. In fact, none of the students in OLA's south wing suffered any serious physical injuries as a result of the fire.

Once they left the school, many kids went with their classes to the safety and warmth of the nearby Our Lady of the Angels Church. They filled the pews until teachers heard rumors that the church was on fire too. It wasn't, but the teachers couldn't be sure, so they told kids to go home.

Some kids ran straight home or to nearby houses or businesses. But many kids joined the hundreds of parents, neighbors, and other adults who watched in horror as firemen and police battled the blaze and tried to rescue more children. Others searched the crowd, calling for brothers, sisters, cousins, and friends. A few ran back into the burning building to find someone they thought was trapped. (At least one boy reportedly died after he ran back inside to look for his little sister, who was already outside.)

The crowd outside the school kept growing. Newspaper, television, and radio reporters followed sirens and police radio reports to OLA, where they quickly saw this fire would become one of the biggest and saddest news stories in Chicago's history. Even the toughest reporters—men who had covered deaths on the battlefields of World War II—were shaken by the sight of children crying for help at their classroom windows. After hearing back from reporters, at least one Chicago radio station abandoned regular programming and played somber music, punctuated only by updates on the fire.

Despite their own horror, most reporters pressed on and sought out kids who could describe what had happened inside the building. Johnnie Montedore, still missing a shoe, told a couple of television news reporters how he had gotten out of the building. The reporters then asked Johnnie and another boy to come down to the television station so they could tell their stories on the air. (In those early days of television, most news cameras could film only silent movies outside; people often had to go to the station's broadcast studio for live interviews.)

Giggling at the prospect of being on TV, the boys said, "Wow, yeah!" After they were in the reporters' car, though, they remembered how they had always been warned against getting into cars with strangers. The boys eyed the men in the front seat nervously and wondered, *Who are these guys? Are they really reporters? Maybe they're kidnappers!*

"All of a sudden we were afraid," Johnnie says.

The reporters evidently noticed the mood change in the back seat. They told the boys not to worry, a local anchorman would interview them on live television. In the meantime, the reporters said, they would call the boys' parents.

Sure enough, when Johnnie and the other boy got to the station, the reporters took them to a television studio, where they told their stories under bright lights for three different broadcasts. (The boys later learned that their interviews were broadcast all over the country. One aunt even saw and heard Johnnie from her home in San Diego, California.)

While the boys were on the air, the reporters called their parents' home phones. No one answered, and no one had cell phones in those days, so the reporters asked for other numbers they could try. Johnnie gave them another aunt's phone number, but no one answered the phone at her house either.

The reason no one answered a phone: Johnnie's entire family was out looking for him. When they first heard about the fire, his parents had raced to the school. When they couldn't find him there, they recruited other family members to go from house to house and from hospital to hospital. Still no Johnnie.

When his parents returned to their apartment around 10 o'clock that night, they thought Johnnie was dead. They did not know that their son had been on television all evening and was now eating dinner with reporters at a Chicago steak house.

A short time later, the reporters brought Johnnie home. "When I knocked on the door, it was sort of a mixed blessing," he says. "My dad didn't know whether to hit me or hug me."

Johnnie's story wasn't unusual. Well, maybe his gig on national television was a little extraordinary. But throughout the OLA neighborhood, survivors and their families were looking for each other. Some kids, such as six-year-old Danny Plovanich, were simply too young to find their way home by themselves. And some, such as Johnna Mass Uting, were registered wrong at the hospital where they were taken. (In the confusion of so many young patients arriving at once, someone at the hospital listed Johnna's name as John, so she was counted as a boy and not included in the hospital's list of girls.)

These mistakes were eventually sorted out. Families looked in the crowds near the school, at nearby homes, in local hospitals, and everywhere else they could think of. For some, their searches ended at the morgue.

OUT OF THE ASHES

I hope something may come out of this
to save lives in the future, not only in Chicago
but throughout the country.
—Cook County coroner Walter McCarron

iremen were still battling the blaze when an OLA priest told a newspaper reporter that he feared as many as 25 children had died in the fire. He was wrong. Eighty-seven students and three teachers died that day. Five more kids would die during the weeks and months ahead.

Altogether, the fire claimed 95 lives: 55 girls, 37 boys, and 3 teachers. Almost 100 more were injured severely enough to be hospitalized.

Why did the fire claim so many more girls than boys? Some firemen later said it had been easier to save boys because, in the last seconds before flames consumed a classroom, a fireman standing outside on a ladder could reach inside a window and grab a boy by his belt. The uniform for OLA girls was a jumper that had nothing to grab.

The city and the nation were shocked. Four days after the fire, the *Chicago American* devoted its entire front page to individual photographs of kids who had died in the fire. The headline on the page read, CHICAGO MOURNS.

Along with grief came questions: What had caused the fire? Why had it spread so quickly? What could be done to prevent similar tragedies in the future? Everyone wanted to know, and cities as far away as London, England, sent fire experts to learn what they could from the tragedy.

As investigators began sifting through the water-soaked rubble, they soon figured out that the fire had started in a basement stairwell. But it wasn't clear *why* it had started.

Rumors flew around Chicago. Some people said the OLA basement had been a mess, filled with trash that could easily catch fire. (Most OLA students knew this wasn't true; they remembered how fastidious Jim

The *Chicago American* devoted its front page to most of the fire victims on December 5, 1958, the day on which many funerals were held.

Raymond had been in keeping the school clean. Nevertheless, rumors of sloppy housekeeping followed the janitor for the rest of his life.) Some people guessed that the school's boilers had exploded or that faulty electrical wiring had sparked the fire. Others thought some kids had been secretly smoking in the basement stairwell.

A few people suspected arson—that someone had deliberately set the fire. But who would set fire to a school filled with children? And how? There was no evidence that gasoline or anything else had been splashed around the stairwell where the fire had started.

Investigators questioned more than 600 students and teachers who had survived. They asked who had left their classrooms in the minutes before the fire. Had any of these students acted suspiciously? Were any of them known to smoke cigarettes? Or to have a fascination with fire?

Nine days after the fire, Cook County coroner Walter McCarron—the man responsible for investigating suspicious deaths in Chicago and its surrounding county—assembled a special jury to begin a public inquest, or investigation, of the OLA fire. "This is a dark page in Chicago's history," Coroner McCarron said. "I hope

A Chicago fireman searches through the school's rubble, looking for clues that could tell how the fire started and why it spread so fast.

something may come out of this to save lives in the future, not only in Chicago but throughout the country."

Sixteen members of a special jury studied the fire scene and listened to the testimony of 22 witnesses. But the jury did not establish the cause of the blaze. Neither did any of the other official investigations of the fire. Almost 60 years later, the cause of the OLA fire was still officially undetermined, and it will almost surely remain so.

But investigators had their suspicions. (See sidebar on page 100.)

The jury did learn what caused the fire to spread so rapidly and so dangerously. In a report at a national conference almost three months later, the jurors identified almost 30 fire-safety problems at OLA and made recommendations for other schools to follow. Here are their most important recommendations:

◆ *Provide automatic sprinkler systems for all school buildings.* Automatic sprinkler systems detect fires and spray water on them. A sprinkler system could have put out the fire in the trash barrel before it spread to the rest of the building.

◆ *Use flame-resistant material to build and enclose school stairs and stairwells.* Fire experts say every material burns if it's hot enough, but some materials—like concrete—resist burning longer than others. OLA's waxed wooden stairs burned quickly, turning stairwells into chimneys that carried heat and fire to the top floor.

◆ *Separate stairwells from hallways and classrooms with fire-resistant doors.* OLA had no fire doors on the second floor. Hal Bruno—then a *Chicago American* reporter who also happened to be a volunteer firefighter at the school on the day of the fire—later explained how serious those missing fire doors were. "If there had been a fire door at the top of those stairs," Mr. Bruno said, "nobody would have died. All they would have had was a trash fire in the stairwell."

◆ *Never prop open fire doors with wedges or blocks.* A propped-open fire door is the same as having no fire door at all. The inquest jury recommended making it a crime to prop open a fire door, especially in a school. (Today some buildings have fire doors that stay open but are equipped with sensors that automatically close the doors if temperatures get too hot. Even these doors, though, do not work properly when wedges or blocks are used.)

HOW DID THE FIRE START?

No one has ever determined *officially* how the fire at Our Lady of the Angels started. Some people think the fire was started by a neighborhood boy who, because of other crimes, spent most of his life in prison. But many other people believe the fire was started by an OLA fifth grader.

Three years after the fire, when he was being investigated for starting other fires in the Chicago area, the boy told police that he had also started the one at Our Lady of the Angels School. The boy said he had been excused from class to go to the bathroom on the afternoon of the fire. While out of his classroom, he said he had dropped three matches into a trash barrel in the school's basement. The boy said he had hoped a fire would close school for a few days.

When the boy's stepfather heard about the confession, he was furious at the police for questioning the boy when neither of his parents was present. After the boy's mother and stepfather talked with him, the boy changed his story and denied starting the OLA fire. Police still believed he had done it because he knew details that had not been made public.

A family court judge later found the boy guilty of starting several fires, but not the one at OLA. Some people said the judge was a devout Catholic who did not want to blame a Catholic school for failing to supervise one of its students. Others said the judge hesitated to make a 10-year-old boy responsible for a tragedy that could haunt him for the rest of his life.

The judge sent the boy to a detention center in Michigan. From there, he grew up to become a soldier and, later, a truck driver. He continued to deny setting the OLA fire until his death in 2004.

◆ *Eliminate glass transoms over classroom doors.* In the 1950s most old schools used transoms to bring air into stuffy classrooms, but the OLA fire showed the danger in those transoms. Even though most of OLA's transoms were closed at the time of the fire, intense heat in the hallways shattered the glass, allowing smoke and flames to pour into classrooms. The jury recommended covering transoms completely and permanently.

◆ *Install automatic fire-alarm systems in schools.* When an automatic alarm system detects smoke, it sounds an alarm in the building and, at the same time, notifies the fire department that there is a fire in the school. On the day of the OLA fire, an automatic alarm system would have eliminated the time people spent looking for telephones and seeking permission to pull the school's manual fire alarm. It also would have eliminated the time firemen wasted going to the wrong address.

◆ *Put fire-alarm boxes within 100 feet of every school.* These boxes, which allow people on the street to call the local fire department, were especially important before people had cell phones. According to the National Fire Protection Association, most school fires are first noticed by someone passing by.

◆ *Treat all school fires as emergencies that require extra rescue workers and equipment.*

◆ *Place fire extinguishers at waist height for adults.* The extinguishers at OLA were all seven feet above the floor—out of the reach of many adults. The inquest jury emphasized that extinguishers should be lower and used by "adult school personnel and custodians" to douse small fires *after* the fire department is called and pupils are exiting the building.

◆ *Eliminate overcrowding.* At the time of the OLA fire, Chicago's fire regulations required 20 square feet of space for each student. If OLA had followed those rules, the top floor of the school's north wing would have been limited to 232 students. Instead, that crowded section of the crowded building held 329 students—97 more kids than would have been allowed in a newer building.

◆ *Eliminate grandfather clauses.* OLA was allowed to put so many students on the top floor because the city's fire code had a grandfather clause that permitted older schools to meet the safety standards that existed at the time they were built. Some fire experts have identified grandfather clauses as the biggest fire hazard in buildings, even in the 21st century.

◆ *Require monthly fire drills in all schools.* OLA had regular fire drills, but many schools did not.

◆ *Make sure exits are clear and doors have panic bars that allow children to push them open quickly.* The kids in the Cheese Box almost died because the door to a fire escape was kept locked, and even kids on OLA's first floor remember fumbling with the school's heavy front doors and worrying that they wouldn't open.

◆ *Use fire-resistant materials to paint, trim, and clean schools.* Many OLA students remember admiring the shine on their old school's wooden floors and staircases. They learned later, though, that the shine came from years of being coated and recoated with varnishes and waxes. The chemicals in those finishes fed the flames.

None of these recommendations surprised fire-safety experts. For years they had been urging public officials to install fire doors, automatic sprinklers, and other safety measures in schools. And for years public officials had agreed these safety measures would be nice but were too expensive for school budgets.

Now, with photographs and stories about the OLA fire splashed across newspapers and featured on television news programs, communities were ready to spend money on keeping children safe. As *Life* magazine pointed out, "The nation woke up to the fact that similar school tragedies could have occurred almost anywhere."

In response to publicity about the OLA fire, state legislatures passed new fire-safety laws, and two-thirds of US cities and towns adopted stricter school fire codes. (The City of New York even closed several schools while workers fixed fire hazards.) Schools installed fire doors, enclosed stairwells, upgraded alarm systems, used fire-resistant building materials, and conducted more frequent fire drills.

This came just as the nation was in the midst of building more schools to accommodate the growing number of baby boomers entering school. As a result of the OLA fire, many plans for two-story buildings were scrapped and replaced with blueprints for one-story buildings. In schools that already existed, firefighters started blocking escape routes during fire drills so students and teachers could practice what to do if smoke and flames kept them from using their normal exit.

"There are no new lessons to be learned from this fire," said Percy Bugbee, the president of the National Fire Protection Association, "only old lessons that tragically went unheeded."

Now, though, everyone was paying attention.

STARTING OVER

Everything that's related to fire safety, put it in there.
—Monsignor William McManus

Besides the children who had been killed, others were hurt. About 100 kids spent time, ranging from a few days to many months, in one of three local hospitals. Some returned again and again for repeated surgeries over the years.

At first doctors teamed up to treat patients, and nurses from other hospitals volunteered time to care for children who'd been injured. Doris Miller, then a head nurse in a surgical unit at nearby Oak Park Hospital, worked an eight-hour shift, without pay, caring for a girl from OLA. The girl later died, but Miss Miller still remembers the special ward set up for OLA burn patients. The kids were wrapped in bandages and forbidden to see their parents except during limited visiting hours. (At the time, such restrictions were routine in hospitals.)

Recoveries were slow and painful. To prevent infection, doctors kept serious burn victims naked on special beds, known as Stryker Frames. The injured kids

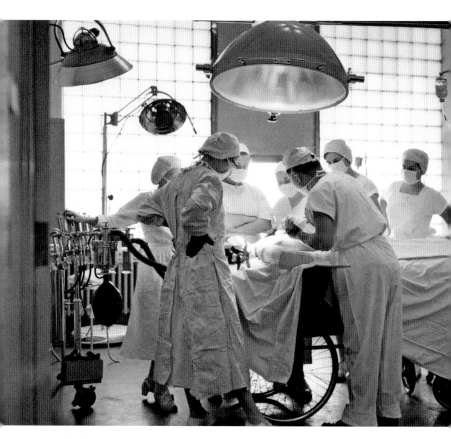

Instead of going home from school the way they expected, many OLA students faced repeated surgeries.

had to be turned every couple of hours, and sometimes they had to face the floor. The threat of infection was so high that anyone entering their rooms—doctors, nurses, and parents—wore sterile masks and gowns. Sometimes even these precautions didn't help. The last OLA fire victim, Bill Edington, died on August 9, 1959, 251 days after the fire.

But was he really the last fire victim?

In the 2000s, survivors' families were still lamenting how their loved ones had suffered, physically and emotionally, their entire lives. Memories of the OLA fire followed them through the years.

In the beginning, the OLA neighborhood grieved each death. Every block lost at least one child in the fire, and some kids served as pallbearers at almost a dozen funerals. Others recall they weren't allowed to attend any services, not even for their best friends.

Some families couldn't bear the sorrow and moved away. The kids who stayed were sent off to other schools while OLA's charred ruins were torn down.

A new school was built on the same spot as the old one. The archdiocesan superintendent, William Mc-Manus, told the new school's architect, "Everything that's related to fire safety, put it in there."

The architect did just that, and the new Our Lady of the Angels School opened in September 1960. Built

The new school building still stands on the footprint of the burned-out OLA.

of concrete and steel, it had state-of-the-art sprinklers, smoke detectors, fire doors, fire-resistant stairwells, alarms that connected to the local firehouse, and a shiny new fire-alarm box in front of the school.

At last, Our Lady of the Angels was a safe school.

Our Lady of the Angels continued to be a safe school until it closed in 1999. By then, its enrollment—once stretched beyond the school's safe capacity with 1,600 students—had shrunk to just 180 students. After OLA left, the building was used at different times for various charter schools. And sometimes the school building stood empty.

The neighborhood, once close-knit and friendly to families, also changed. It began to struggle with gang activity, violence, and extreme poverty. In 2005 the old OLA church became known as the Mission of Our Lady of the Angels, where staff members worked with people in the neighborhood but no longer ran an active parish center. The closest Catholic church was about a mile away.

Some people thought the changes began with the OLA fire, when heartbroken parents moved away and neighbors started lashing out at each other in confusion and grief. But others thought change would have come anyway; it was simply in the air, waiting for the 1960s to begin.

EPILOGUE

AFTERMATH

It certainly brought home the fragility of life.
—Serge Uccetta

In the days after the fire, survivors dealt with feelings of guilt and grief. Why did they get out, and why didn't their friends and classmates?

"It certainly brought home the fragility of life," says Serge Uccetta, who escaped from Room 208. "When you're 12 or 13, who thinks about this stuff? . . . A tragedy of this magnitude shows you the fickleness of life and how things like this can happen. In my case, it was always, *Gee, why did I happen to get out and those other kids didn't?* And there's no answer to that question. It's just that's the way it is."

Even worse was the feeling that the survivors somehow caused the deaths of their classmates. Michele
Barale fixated on the piles of bodies she had climbed
over, on her way to the window in Room 211. "That's
what I remembered for *years and years and years*, with
utter horror and a lot of guilt," she says.

Ron Sarno is also familiar with guilt, after losing his
sister in Room 210 and his older brother in Room 211.
"A lot of friends died too," he says. "Kids that I grew
up with, kids that lived down the block that I used to
play with. But the big thing was my sister. Why didn't
I get her out? Why couldn't I get her out? I think I've
accepted it now—that, hey, I was nine, ten years old.
I probably did the best I could. And it wasn't meant
to be."

In the days right after the fire, the surviving students
suffered alone, without grief counselors or help of any
kind. "We were told that God took the good ones,"
remembers Mike Guzaldo, a survivor of Room 201. If
God took the good ones, what were the ones who had
survived?

No one would say. "We never talked about the fire
at school," says Carol Vinceri Woodall, who had left
her seventh-grade classroom to help the first graders.
"We were just supposed to clam up and go on with
our lives."

THE END OF FUNNY

———

Billy and Joanne Sarno

Billy and Joanne Sarno both died in the fire at OLA. Billy was an eighth grader in Room 211, and Joanne was a fourth grader in Room 210. These photos, along with the photo of their brother Ron on page 39, were taken a few weeks before the fire.

Ron says his parents were never the same after two of their children died. Their father,

continued on next page ...

for instance, "used to be a jokester," Ron remembers, but the fire "seemed to change his whole demeanor." Life was no longer funny.

Ron's father was not alone. The entire neighborhood began to change with the loss of so many children and their teachers. Every block around OLA had lost at least one child, so everyone had reason to mourn. And maybe move away.

Carol says her teacher was one of the nuns who helped rescue kids during the fire. But once everyone was back in school, even that teacher was emphatic: "We were never to talk about the fire again," Carol remembers. "If she even heard one word [about the fire], we were reprimanded for saying it. We desperately wanted to talk about it since we all had friends and family who perished in the fire. But we never knew exactly what happened."

Other teachers also enforced silence about the fire. "We were not allowed to talk about the fire or about anybody who'd died or about anybody who was in the hospital," says Kathy Galante Guisinger, a Cheese Box survivor. "That was a no-no. You just didn't do it."

No public reminder existed at the fire site until 2007—almost 50 years after the fire—when Cardinal Francis George blessed a new memorial listing the names of the 92 students and three teachers who died in the fire.

Teachers and parents probably thought they were protecting children when they maintained silence about the fire. In a way, they were right; they protected kids from early accounts—such as ones that blamed smoking students or poor housekeeping—that were often wrong. But even correct information was often kept from OLA students. In addition to the school's general ban on discussing the fire, many parents worried that talking about the fire would just increase their children's anxiety.

And parents were dealing with anxieties of their own. Luci Mordini remembers her mother had already been scarred by things that happened in her native country of Italy during World War II. The fire at OLA was another "huge trauma," says Luci. "She kind of shut me in from then on. I couldn't ride a bike, I couldn't drive, I couldn't date, I couldn't do anything. Other people will tell you that happened in their families too. I don't think anybody knew how to handle anything of this magnitude. If you look at the number of families affected, it was in the hundreds."

Between school and home, almost everyone was troubled but quiet about the fire. Indeed, many survivors say they heard so little about the fire that they did not learn exactly what had happened until they grew up and began to read factual accounts of the event for themselves.

In the meantime, the kids developed a passion for fire safety. They remember worrying, for instance, about the height of the schools they attended while OLA was being rebuilt. How would they get out, in case of fire?

Even today, many say they look for and stay near clearly marked exits in everything from meeting rooms to movie theaters. "When I stay in a hotel—and I do a lot of travel for business—I make sure I go from my room to where the exits are," says Michele Barale. "I won't stay too high up."

Neither will Ron Sarno, who survived the jump from his classroom. "Even today," he says, "when I go into a hotel, I ask for a room on the lower level. I always plan my route of escape."

But it's not just the jumpers who have become careful about identifying exits. Becky Morrissey Ruhland walked safely with other fourth graders out of their basement classroom, but she's still nervous about finding exits. "When I go to a new place," she says, "the first thing I do is look for an exit. I want to know where it is."

Several OLA students took their interest in school fire safety into careers as firefighters or security experts. Others championed school safety measures. Johnna Mass Uting Bovenzo argued with a principal and testified before a school board to get the padlocks removed from an exit at her son's school. The fire at OLA taught Johnna that the worst imaginable things *can* happen. "So I'm gonna fight for the kids," she says.

Even if they didn't become professional firefighters or vocal advocates, OLA survivors became very quick about responding to fire alarms. They'd learned how fast fire travels, so "if you heard a fire alarm, you got the heck out of there," says Carol Vinceri Woodall. "You're overly sensitive."

After the fire, OLA kids certainly paid attention to fire drills. Most schools now hold them monthly, just as the National Fire Protection Association recommends. But as the OLA tragedy has faded from memories, school fire drills have often become more of a fun break than serious practice for a life-threatening emergency.

Even teachers often don't take fire drills seriously, says Pam Krajecke Pultorak, who became a school secretary after surviving the OLA fire as a second grader. "A fire drill means nothing to most teachers. Nothing," she says. "Half of them don't close their doors [when they leave their classrooms during a drill]. They don't take an attendance book, they don't count heads, and they don't know when a kid is missing."

Matt Plovanich, who escaped the Cheese Box just before it blew up, thinks today's teachers and students just don't understand "how quickly fire travels and how quickly things deteriorate. There is not a lot of time to contemplate. That's what I tell my kids all the time. You basically have to have a plan in place before it happens.

am Krajecke (center), a few weeks after the fire, with her aunt and aby cousin.

That's why you want to size up your surroundings, look for exits, look for an escape route ahead of time, because once that fire starts, conditions deteriorate quickly."

Matt has run practice fire drills and posed what-ifs with his own kids. When the family moved to a new house, he lined up everyone and said, "OK, [pretend] this hallway is not passable. How do you get out?"

Remembering how he and his classmates lay on the floor and waited for someone to open the Cheese Box, Matt urges today's kids to take action. "Do whatever it takes to get out," he says. If a fire occurs at home and "your siblings are sleeping, wake them up and get them out of there. If you have a choice of jumping or staying in, if it's that bad, please don't do what I did [in the Cheese Box]. Make sure you jump."

Matt doesn't want kids to worry about breaking anything—like a window—to escape. "Do what you have to do to get out," he says. "Break that window. If it has to be repaired at a later date, you can always repair it."

In the years since the OLA fire, schools have become much safer. Most have enclosed stairwells, automatic sprinklers, and connections to fire departments. But when he visits schools, Matt is still disturbed by the fire doors. "The good news is that schools have fire doors," he says. "The bad news is that they're often chained in the open position. . . . The fire doors are absolutely useless if you keep them open."

The lack of fire doors at OLA still haunts Matt. "Had there been fire doors at the top of our stairwell," he says, "that fire would have been compartmentalized in that stairwell, and it would have extinguished itself. It wouldn't have grown into the monster that eventually took all those lives."

Although schools are much safer today, they're still stuffed with books, computers, heating equipment, and humans who make mistakes. Perhaps the biggest lesson from OLA is learning how quickly things can change, how fragile life is.

Andy Lego says the fire taught him that life can be taken away in a matter of seconds. "I definitely learned that you don't live forever," he says. "You could go tomorrow. And if you go, you can go in 30 seconds."

As a result, Andy says, "I don't take myself very seriously. When I see people taking themselves too seriously, I think, *Ye gods, what have you done? It can all go away in 30 seconds.*"

Matt Plovanich agrees. The fire "changed a lot of things in my world," he says. "I realized that we all have expiration dates. We're like sour cream: We've got a shelf life. We're gonna go. I became an adult awfully quickly. I think there's a certain amount of innocence that went out the window at that point. But I do appreciate life every day since that day. . . . Every day has been great. I don't complain about hangnails."

He confesses exasperation with people who complain about "the most mundane things. If these people only knew . . ."

Michele Barale's takeaway has been a little less philosophical—and a lot simpler. If you're in a fire, she says, "Act. Don't be passive. Don't wait for someone to save you."

In other words, get out.

ACKNOWLEDGMENTS

I went to school in a six-room schoolhouse called West Wayne. All of the classrooms were on one floor in a building that had four exits and four huge windows in each classroom. Although West Wayne's building was old (probably of the same vintage as the original Our Lady of the Angels School in Chicago), its small size and easy access kept it from being a firetrap. Those advantages did not keep the school principal and his secretary (who both taught part time) from worrying about fire, especially after the tragedy at Our Lady of the Angels.

They decided to test everyone by blocking one of the four exits during a fire drill. The principal piled chairs in front of the school's front door, and watched to see what teachers and kids would do.

The fifth-grade teacher, who normally led his class out through the now-blocked door, saw the blockade and quickly figured how to get past it. He took a flying leap at the pile of chairs and sent them scattering in all directions. Fifth graders could then leave by their normal exit—although some had nicked shins or banged heads. The teacher himself had to go home early with injuries that day.

Still, the flying-chairs incident, as it came to be known, seems minor, especially when compared with the horrors at Our Lady of the Angels. But the incident shows how the whole country—even the staff in a six-room public schoolhouse in northern Indiana—was swept up in the OLA tragedy. The flying-chairs incident predicted how and why safety would drive decisions about schools today.

I am grateful to Lisa Reardon for championing *The School's on Fire!*, to Jerry Pohlen for picking up where Lisa left off, to Claudia Wood for asking good questions, to Ellen Hornor for finding the right answers, and to the other helpful folks at Chicago Review Press. I also thank Ann Tobias, Julie Amper, and Jan Smith for their early advice on this book.

Thanks also go to Diana Scheeler for housing and transporting me during my trips to Chicago. I am grateful to Meg Hall and Julie A. Satzik at the Chicago

Archdiocese; Jennifer Head and Angie Connolly at the Sisters of Charity of the Blessed Virgin Mary in Dubuque, Iowa; Sister Stephanie Baliga at the Mission of Our Lady of the Angels in Chicago; and Jack Connors of the Fire Museum of Greater Chicago. Special thanks to Peg O'Brien and Judy Comoletti at the National Fire Protection Association in Boston. I also appreciate the help of Tony Dudek at the *Chicago Tribune* and Tricia Gesner at the Associated Press.

The fire at OLA was a big surprise. Fittingly, I had my own surprise—in the form of a stroke—while working on this manuscript. This delayed the project and made life difficult for my husband, Chris Jones. I want to thank him for the work he has done and the support he has offered while I learned to type and write again.

I also want to thank every single one of the OLA survivors who gave their time generously, willingly relived one of the worst days of their lives, and often dug through old photographs that must have stirred painful memories. I met most of the survivors in this book through olafire.com, a website created by Eric Morgan in 2001. If you have a question about OLA after reading this book, you'll almost surely find the answer at olafire.com.

Finally, I want to thank Jean Hart, who swung out of Room 209, became the teacher who patiently answered my questions, and carefully went over the details in this manuscript. Any errors that remain are, of course, my own.

WHAT TO DO IN CASE OF FIRE

Fires aren't usually as big as the one at Our Lady of the Angels. But a smaller fire can be just as deadly to the person who's caught in it.

House fires are especially dangerous. According to the National Fire Protection Association, almost 80 percent of fire deaths occur in homes. About 2,560 Americans—including about 345 under the age of 15—are killed in house fires every year. Planning what to do ahead of time can save your life.

To be safe, fire-safety experts recommend that you follow a few simple steps:

◆ *Check smoke alarms.* Make sure they work. Batteries should be checked monthly and changed once a year, or when a chirping alarm indicates a low battery. (A good time to change batteries is when your family sets back the time on clocks.) Place a smoke alarm on every floor, near stairwells, and near bedrooms.

◆ *Develop an escape plan.* Pick a meeting place outside the house where people can check on each other in case of fire or emergency. Make sure the meeting place is close to the house but far enough away to be safe.

◆ *Practice your escape plan.* The National Fire Protection Association recommends involving the whole family in a practice escape twice a year.

◆ *Identify two ways out of each major room*—usually a door and a window.

◆ *Close the bedroom doors at night.* According to the Chicago Fire Department, a closed door can keep out fire and smoke for up to 20 minutes. An open door lets in those killers right away.

◆ *Check doors before opening them.* If the smoke alarm goes off, feel the door with the back of your hand. If the door is hot, don't open it. You can leave through the window if you're on the first floor. If you're higher, blow a whistle, scream, or make any loud sound. Wave a pillowcase, shirt, or some other cloth for attention. *Don't hide!*

◆ *Crawl.* If the smoke alarm goes off in the middle of the night, roll out of bed and crawl under the smoke. Keep crawling until you reach the meeting place outside.

◆ *Don't waste time.* Fires move fast, so you have to move fast too. Don't hide, don't grab valuables, don't try to save pets, and don't use elevators. Just get out.

◆ *Go to the meeting place. Do not go back inside— for any reason.* Tell a firefighter if you know someone is still inside.

◆ *Call 911.* If firefighters aren't already there, call 911 from your meeting place—or from a neighbor's house.

LEARN MORE

BOOKS

You can read and learn more about the OLA fire in the following books:

Chiappetta, Robert. *The Immaculate Deception.* New York: Page Publishing, 2015. Robert Chiappetta's sister died in the fire.

Cowan, David, and John Kuenster. *To Sleep with the Angels: The Story of a Fire.* Chicago: Ivan R. Dee, 1996. This is the go-to book for information about the fire and its investigation.

Kern, Elizabeth. *Fire Angels: A Novel.* Chicago: Chicago Review Press, 2016.

Kuenster, John. *Remembrances of the Angels: 50th Anniversary Reminiscences of the Fire No One Can Forget.* Chicago: Ivan R. Dee, 2008.

McBride, Michele. *The Fire That Will Not Die.* Palm Springs, CA: ETC Publications, 1979. McBride, now deceased, was injured in the fire.

Verstraete, Larry. *Survivors! True Death-Defying Escapes.* New York: Scholastic, 2004.

NEWSPAPERS AND MAGAZINES

More good information can be found in practically any US newspaper in December 1958. At the time, Chicago had four daily newspapers—the *Tribune*, the *Daily News*, the *Sun-Times*, and the *American*—and they all carried heartbreaking details about Our Lady of the Angels.

Many magazines have told the story of the fire. Here are some of particular interest:

Babcock, Chester I., and Rexford Wilson. "The Chicago School Fire." *The Quarterly* (a publication of the National Fire Protection Association), January 1959.

Cowan, David. "Haunted by Angels." *Chicago*, December 1993.

Greene, Daniel. "Tragedy in the Parish." *Chicago History*, Spring 2001.

Groves, Adam. "Our Lady of the Angels School Fire: 50 Years Later." *Fire Engineering*, December 2008.

Hoy, Suellen. "Stunned with Sorrow." *Chicago History*, Summer 2004.

Life. "Anguish the Nation Shares." December 15, 1958.

OTHER

Angels Too Soon: The 1958 Fire at Our Lady of the Angels School. Chicago: WTTW. This Emmy Award–winning program, originally produced for WTTW in Chicago, can now be purchased as a DVD from the station.

Cook County Coroner's Jury Report. Chicago, IL. December 10–15, 1958.

"Findings and Recommendations of the Cook County Coroner's Jury." Presentation at a fire department instructors' conference. Memphis, TN. February 24–27, 1959. www.olafire.com/coroner.asp.

You can find many articles, documents, photographs, and interesting conversations at www.olafire.com.

NOTES

PROLOGUE: FIRE ALARM!

"I had the feeling": Carol Vinceri Woodall, telephone interview with the author, July 24, 2007.

"Well, that's strange": Woodall interview.

CHAPTER 1: THE STAIRWELL

"I figured it was so big": James Raymond, Testimony to Cook County Coroner's Jury, December 11, 1958.

"The school next door": David Cowan and John Kuenster, *To Sleep with the Angels: The Story of a Fire* (Chicago: Ivan R. Dee, 1996), 32.

"Our Lady of the Angels School": Cowan and Kuenster, *Sleep with the Angels*, 33.

"Somebody called it in": Cowan and Kuenster, 33.

CHAPTER 2: ROOM 208

"It's really hot in here": Luciana Mordini, statement recalled and told to author, telephone interview, December 6, 2007.

"Then it was like a": Serge Uccetta, telephone interview with the author, June 28, 2007.

"The heck with this": Andy Lego, statement recalled and told to author, telephone interview, June 28, 2007.

"I can still see the flames": Lego interview.

"Please, bring the ladder": Uccetta interview.

"I thought I was going to die": OLA fire survivor posting at www.olafire.com/Survivors.asp#208.

"I was sitting on the window frame": Mordini interview.

CHAPTER 3: ROOM 207: THE CHEESE BOX

"Sister, I see smoke": Matthew Plovanich, statement recalled in telephone interview with the author, November 8, 2008.

"I will never forget the look": Matthew Plovanich interview.

"Help! Help!": Matthew Plovanich, statements recalled in interview.

"Hail Mary, full of grace": Traditional Catholic prayer.

"I really did not have": Matthew Plovanich interview.

"I thought to myself": Kathleen Galante Guisinger, telephone interview with the author, July 5, 2007.

"I had my head down": Matthew Plovanich interview.

"I began to cry": Matthew Plovanich, statements recalled in interview.

"I don't think I ever saw": Matthew Plovanich interview.

"The school is on fire!": Guisinger interview.

"Smoke was just pouring out": Matthew Plovanich interview.

"Look at you!": Matthew Plovanich, recollection of conversation with his mother in interview.

CHAPTER 4: ROOM 210

"but I didn't understand": Ron Sarno, telephone interview with the author, January 30, 2008.

"Sister was gathering us": Connie Bellino, telephone interview with the author, February 8, 2009.

"was crazy, just chaos": Sarno interview.

"Don't jump!": Sarno, statements recalled in interview.

"We were standing at the window": Sarno interview.

"Part of me thinks": Bellino interview.

"You have no idea": Bellino, statement recalled in interview.

"She told the kids": Sarno interview.

"God helps those": Bellino interview.

CHAPTER 5: ROOM 209

"Sister, it's hotter than": Rosemary Pisani Bieker, conversation recalled in telephone interview with the author, January 27, 2009.

"OK, open the door": Bieker, statements recalled in interview.

"I don't remember being": Andrew D'Amore, telephone interview with the author, undated.

"Sister did not want everyone": Bieker interview.

"Call to them!": Bieker, statement recalled in interview.

"The school's on fire": Bieker, statement recalled in interview.

"In my brain": Jean Hart, telephone interview with the author, January 29, 2009.

"Rose, wait!": Cowan and Kuenster, *Sleep with the Angels*, 48–49.

"When the wall": Hart interview.

CHAPTER 6: ROOM 211

"Obviously, it wasn't a real heavy": Edward Glanz, telephone interview with the author, May 5, 2009.

"Sister, the school is on fire!": Glanz, statement recalled in interview.

"like cords of wood": John Lubke, telephone interview with the author, May 11, 2009.

This can't be happening: Michele Barale, telephone interview with the author, March 10, 2009.

"Cover your heads!": Barale, statement recalled in interview.

"There were all the big, tall": Barale interview.

"Wait for me!": Barale, statement recalled in interview.

I'm not waiting: Barale interview.

CHAPTER 7: ROOM 212

Oh, those firemen!: Johnna Mass Uting Bovenzo, telephone interview with the author, February 19, 2009.

"there was not a lot of screaming": John Raymond, telephone interview with the author, December 11, 2008.

"Everybody stay in your seats": Bovenzo, statement recalled in interview.

"Sister, Sister, what do": Bovenzo, conversation recalled in interview.

"The heat was so intense": Bovenzo interview.

"I just sat there": Raymond interview.

CHAPTER 8: THE ANNEX

"I vividly remember a first-grade teacher": Mike Ramelli, telephone interview with the author, February 11, 2009.

CHAPTER 9: THE REST OF THE BUILDING

"Oh my God!": Dan Plovanich, statement recalled in telephone interview with the author, November 28, 2008.

"still a little unsure": Dan Plovanich interview.

"stampede-shuffle": www.olafire.com.

"You could barely see": John Montedore, telephone interview with the author, August 27, 2009.

"Ooh, we're not going": Montedore, statement recalled in interview.

"Wow, yeah!": Montedore, statement recalled in interview.

"All of a sudden": Montedore interview.

CHAPTER 10: OUT OF THE ASHES

"This is a dark page": Walter McCarron, opening remarks, coroner's inquest, December 10, 1958.

"If there had been a fire door": Hal Bruno, *Angels Too Soon*, WTTW.

"adult school personnel": "Findings and Recommendations of the Cook County Coroner's Jury," presentation at a fire department instructors' conference (Memphis, TN: February 24–27, 1959).

"The nation woke up": "Anguish the Nation Shares," *Life*, December 15, 1958, 23.

"There are no new lessons": Hal Bruno, "Old Lessons Continue to Go Unheeded," Firehouse, March 31, 2003, www.firehouse.com/leadership/article/10545021 /old-lessons-continue-to-go-unheeded.

CHAPTER 11: STARTING OVER

"Everything that's related to fire safety": Cowan and Kuenster, *Sleep with the Angels*, 246.

EPILOGUE: AFTERMATH

"It certainly brought home": Uccetta interview.

"That's what I remembered": Barale interview.

"A lot of friends died": Sarno interview.

"used to be a jokester": Ron Sarno, email exchange with the author, May 19, 2017.

"We were told that God": Mike Guzaldo, telephone interview with the author, February 12, 2012.

"We never talked about the fire": Woodall interview.

"We were not allowed to talk": Guisinger interview.

"huge trauma": Mordini interview.

"When I stay in a hotel": Barale interview.

"Even today": Sarno interview.

"When I go to a new place": Rebecca Morrissey Ruhland, telephone interview with the author, undated.

"So I'm gonna fight": Bovenzo interview.

"if you heard a fire alarm": Woodall interview.

"A fire drill means nothing": Pam Krajecke Pultorak, telephone interview with the author, undated.

"how quickly fire travels": Matthew Plovanich interview.

"I definitely learned": Lego interview.

"changed a lot of things": Matthew Plovanich interview.

"Act. Don't be passive": Barale interview.

PEOPLE INTERVIEWED
FOR THIS BOOK

Sister Stephanie Baliga
Michele Barale
Connie Bellino
Rosemary Pisani Bieker
Johnna Mass Uting
  Bovenzo
Andrew D'Amore
Ed Glanz (now deceased)
Kathleen Galante
  Guisinger
Mike Guzaldo
Jean Hart
Andrew Lego
John Lubke
Rev. John McNalis

John Montedore
Luciana Mordini
Joyce Peneschi (now
  deceased)
Dan Plovanich
Matthew Plovanich
Pamela Krajecke Pultorak
Michael Ramelli
John Raymond
Rebecca Morrissey
  Ruhland
Ronald Sarno
Doris Miller Turner
Serge Uccetta
Carol Vinceri Woodall

IMAGE CREDITS

Page 3: Courtesy of the Fire Museum of Greater Chicago

Page 6: Archdiocese of Chicago's Joseph Cardinal Bernardin Archives and Records Center

Page 10: Courtesy of Jean Hart

Page 14–15: Based on map provided by Eric Morgan of olafire.com; redrawn by Lindsey Cleworth Schauer

Page 18: Courtesy of Serge Uccetta

Page 23: Courtesy of Luciana Mordini

Page 30: Courtesy of Matthew Plovanich

Page 34–35: Associated Press

Page 39: Courtesy of Ron Sarno

Page 47: Courtesy of Rosemary Pisani Bieker

Page 53: Courtesy of Jean Hart

Page 61: Courtesy of the Fire Museum of Greater Chicago

Page 64–65: Courtesy of the Fire Museum of Greater Chicago

Page 73: Courtesy of Johnna Mass Uting Bovenzo

Page 83: Courtesy of Dan Plovanich

Page 85: Courtesy of Mike Guzaldo

Page 95: © 1958 All rights reserved. Distributed by Tribune Content Agency, LLC

Page 97: Courtesy of the Fire Museum of Greater Chicago

Page 108: © 1958 All rights reserved. Distributed by Tribune Content Agency, LLC

Page 110: Courtesy of the Mission of Our Lady of the Angels

Page 115: Courtesy of Billy and Joanne's brother, Ron Sarno

Page 117: Courtesy of the Mission of Our Lady of the Angels

Page 121: Courtesy of Pamela Krajecke Pultorek

INDEX